Latin
COOKING

RICARDO OLIVAREZ

HACKBERRY PRESS

A QUANTUM BOOK

Published by
Hackberry Press, a division of The Texas Bookman
2700 Lone Star Drive
Dallas
Texas 75212
USA

This edition printed 2003

ISBN 1-931040-26-5

QUMLTC

This book is produced by
Quantum Publishing Ltd
6 Blundell Street
London N7 9BH

Typeset in Great Britain by
Central Southern Typesetters, Eastbourne
Manufactured in Singapore by
Bright Arts (Pte) Ltd.
Printed in Singapore by
Star Standard Industries (Pte) Ltd.

Picture Credits:
p.6, top left, bottom left and right, Peter Wilson; p.8, top left, Peter Wilson.

Material in this publication previously appeared in: **Mexican Main Dishes**, Marlena Spieler; **Nuevo Cubano**, Sue Mullin; **Mexican Cooking**, Roger Hicks; **Creole Cooking**, Sue Mullin; **Caribbean Cooking,** Devinia Sookia; **Spanish Cooking**, Pepita Aris; **Tapas,** Adrian Lissen with Sara Cleary; **Salsa,** Marjie Lambert.

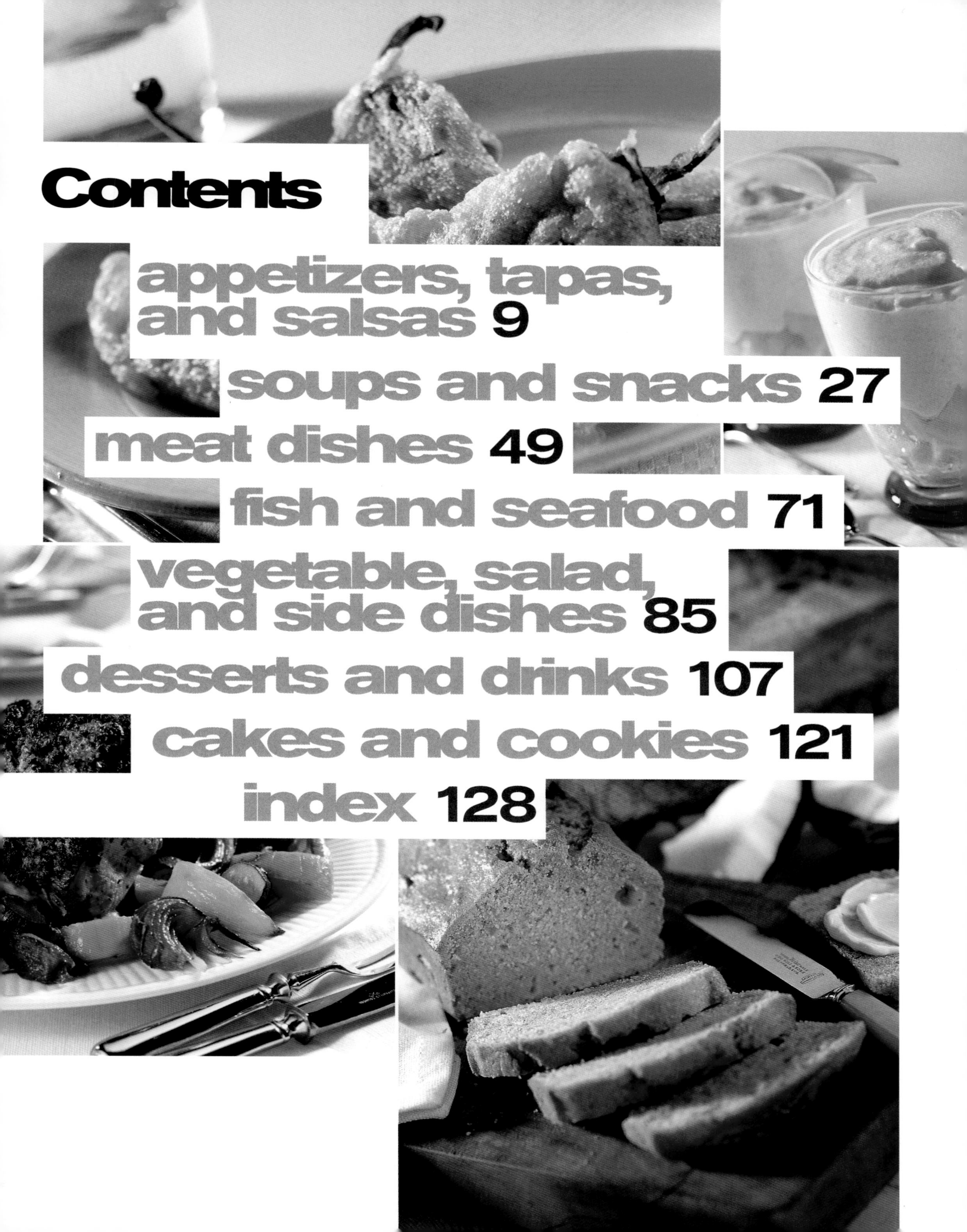

Contents

Introduction

The recipes on the pages that follow represent the diverse and exciting cuisine that is described as "Latin." The dishes are drawn from Spain itself and from those areas of Central America and the Caribbean that were originally explored and settled by the Spanish.

Some common themes are evident—tapas are found in both Europe and the Americas—as is the use of fresh produce, especially fish and in-season vegetables, in all the recipes. Nevertheless, despite some obvious cross-fertilization of styles and ingredients, individual dishes are largely true to a local, rather than an international or even national tradition.

Following is a brief guide to some of the less often encountered ingredients that you will need to complete the recipes. Where relevant, easily obtainable alternatives are suggested, but remember that half the fun of cooking comes from trying new tastes and textures, so do experiment with some of the less familiar ingredients.

These days we see more and more exotic fruits and vegetables in our shops. Plantain, cassava (yuca), coconut, mango, avocado, star fruit (carambola), guava, papaya, and pineapple are no longer available only in specialty markets, but can be found in most supermarkets. Fish merchants no longer stock only sole, snapper, and trout. As with all cooking, use only fresh, good quality ingredients. Avoid fruit with bruised and damaged skin and leaves that look limp and tired. Select fish that looks bright and clean. Buy meat from a butcher, who will be able to advise you on the most suitable cuts for your needs, and avoid precut, prewrapped supermarket fare.

On the whole, you will need no special kitchen equipment. However, many of the dishes include sauces and marinades that contain acidic ingredients such as lime juice and vinegar, so make sure you use non-reactive mixing bowls and casseroles to prevent pitting.

Fish

Flying fish, which has a white, slightly salty flesh, is found off the coast of Barbados.
Grouper There are more than 50 varieties of grouper, a predatory fish found in the waters off the Florida coast. The moist, firm flesh tastes rather like sea bass, which is a good substitute.
Marlin, a game fish, has firm, dense flesh with a rich flavor. It is ideal for barbecuing and cooking on the broiler and for frying.
Pompano has delicate white flesh. It is more expensive than other fish—sole is a good substitute. Fillets are thin but they are full of flavor.
Red snapper is abundantly available in the waters off Cuba and the coast of Florida, and it is one of the most useful of all fish. Similar to grouper and sea bass, red snapper has a lean but firm flesh with a distinctive flavor.
Conch is the meat inside the beautiful spiral-shaped shells.

Vegetables

Ackee is the fruit of an evergreen tree. When the reddish-yellow fruit is ripe it bursts open to reveal shiny black seeds covered by a creamy-yellow flesh—the only edible section. The fruit must only be eaten ripe—unripe and overripe ackee are toxic. Ackee is used in a variety of savory dishes—and the canned variety is a perfectly adequate alternative.
Boniatos are white-fleshed, sweet potatoes. The texture is similar to that of white potatoes, but they have a more subtle, spicy sweetness than the vivid orange sweet potato.
Breadfruit is a large round or oval fruit used as a vegetable, best used when green. Remove central core before boiling, roasting, or frying the cream-colored, starchy flesh.
Cassava also called yuca, manioc, tapioca, and mandioca, is a large starchy tuber, whose tough skin looks like bark. Even when you have cut through the skin, you still have to cut away the fibrous cord that runs through the center. Widely used throughout the Caribbean.
Chiles vary in hotness, but you must always be very careful when you handle them—they can burn the skin and irritate the eyes—so always wear rubber gloves when preparing them.
Christophene is a pear-shaped, squash-like fruit with a single large stone in the center. The skin varies from white to pale yellow to bright green, and the flesh, which tastes something like zucchini with a slight citrus tang, is treated as a vegetable.
Dasheen is another tuberous vegetable, which is used in a variety of recipes. The leaves, poisonous unless cooked, are best known when combined with coconut milk and lime in the soup that bears their other name, callaloo. If not available, use fresh spinach.
Malanga, which is called *yautia* in Puerto Rico, is a large, knobbly tuber. Native to the Americas, it has an unusual nutty flavor, which is widely appreciated in Cuba and Puerto Rico. If you are using white potatoes instead of malanga, add about 1 teaspoon of ground walnuts for every 4 ounces of potato in order to approximate the unique flavor of malanga.
Plantains are the "big brothers" of the banana family, but they must always be cooked and can, therefore, be regarded as vegetables.

Clockwise from top left to bottom left: fishing boats, Sesimbra, Portugal; conch; sea bass; red snapper; dried chiles; bakery, Venezuela; tapas bar sign, Anadalucia, Spain.

Fruit

Avocado commonly known as pear throughout the Caribbean.
Guava is grown in many parts of the world, including Australia, South Africa, and Southeast Asia, as well as Central America. The fruit, which is walnut- to apple-sized, has lots of edible seeds embedded in the pulp. Test for ripeness as you would a pear.
Mamey sapotes come from a very large family. Look out for real mamey sapotes, which have rough, brownish skins.
Mango Most types of mango turn from green to various shades of yellow, orange, and red as they ripen. Select as for melons.
Papayas called *fruta bomba* in Cuba, or pawpaws, are cultivated throughout the year. This avocado-shaped, thin-skinned delight is usually sold green, hard, and unripe. To ripen, place the fruit in a heavy, brown paper bag, perforated with a few holes. After a few days at room temperature, the papaya will ripen to a rosy-yellow.
Passion fruit The skin of passion fruit is sometimes a musty brown color, and the fruit inside has lots of edible seeds in the pulp.
Plantain A fruit of the banana family, similar in shape but larger and not so sweet. Can be green or yellow in color according to ripeness.
Star fruit, sometimes also called carambola, has a waxy yellow or white skin with five ribs. Decorative when sliced.

Flavorings

Allspice is in fact an individual spice, derived from the dried berry of the pimento tree. Use allspice to gee up rather bland foods.
Cilantro, a herb, has a broad, flat, serrated leaf. Do not confuse fresh cilantro with ground coriander, which is derived from the seed.
Tamarind is the fruit of the tamarind tree and comes in long, seed-studded pods, which look like gigantic brown peapods. The tangy brown pulp inside is edible, and it is used in many Latin dishes. Frozen or dried pulp is available in some specialty stores.
Vanilla is derived from a tropical orchid, whose beans are cured and fermented to produce the volatile oil. Sometimes used whole.

Finally, a word about **coconut milk**, which is used in several of the recipes.
Coconut milk, which should not be confused with the juice inside the fresh fruit, was originally made by painstakingly grating the kernel and mixing it with a little water. There are a number of excellent brands of canned coconut milk, both sweetened and unsweetened, available, which will save you time and effort.

Clockwise from top left: Southern Mexico; plantain; avocado; star fruit; cilantro; allspice.

appetizers, tapas, and salsas

Serves 3–4

homemade nachos

Homemade nachos are easy to make, and with real cheese and lots of extras they're better than most commercial versions. The joy of homemade nachos is that you can prepare them to suit your own taste. This deluxe version calls for tomatoes, avocados, olives, green onions, and salsa.

Ingredients

10–12-oz bag of tortilla chips
3 cups grated Cheddar or Jack cheese, or a combination
2 or 3 jalapeño chiles, fresh or canned, cut crosswise into thin slices
2 medium tomatoes, seeded and chopped
⅓ cup chopped green onions
⅓–½ cup black olives, pitted and sliced
1 large ripe avocado, peeled, pitted, and diced, or Avocado Salsa or Guacamole
1 cup tomato-based salsa

Preheat the oven to 400°F. Mound the chips on 1–2 oven-safe serving platters, layering with the cheese and jalapeños. Bake for 3–5 minutes, until the cheese is melted.

Remove from the oven and sprinkle with the tomatoes, green onions, olives, and avocados. Serve with salsa on the side.

Serves 4

Serve this flavorful spread on toast points with cocktails at dinner parties. It can be made the day before and is guaranteed no-muss, no-fuss.

smoked marlin spread

Coarsely chop the fish and place it in a mixing bowl.

Add the relish, horseradish, onion, and lime juice and mix well. Add half the hot-pepper sauce and half the mayonnaise. Blend together and taste.

Add more hot-pepper sauce according to taste, and add salt and pepper to taste.

The spread should be quite thick. Add more mayonnaise only if needed.

Ingredients

8 oz smoked marlin
4 level Tbsp sweet pickle relish
2 Tbsp prepared horseradish
2 Tbsp chopped onion
¼ tsp freshly squeezed lime juice
½ tsp hot-pepper sauce or to taste
up to 6 Tbsp mayonnaise
salt and freshly ground black pepper

Serves 4

Grouper spread is usually eaten on crackers. It also makes a delicious dip for crudités. Any white-fleshed fillet, such as halibut, whitefish, or snapper, can be substituted or, in a pinch, use drained canned pink salmon.

smoked grouper spread

In a blender or food processor, combine the grouper, cream cheese, lime juice, onion, horseradish, and liquid smoke. Process until smooth.

Stir in the walnuts and parsley or cilantro. Transfer to a crock or heavy small bowl.

Cover and refrigerate until ready to serve.

Ingredients

7 oz cooked grouper, any bones or skin removed
1 cup cream cheese, softened
1 Tbsp freshly squeezed lime juice
1 Tbsp grated onion
1 tsp prepared horseradish
¼ tsp liquid smoke
½ cup chopped walnuts
3 Tbsp chopped fresh parsley or cilantro

Serves 4

Ingredients

2 onions, finely chopped
1 large sweet green bell pepper, seeded and diced
5 garlic cloves, mashed
½ cup olive oil
4-oz jar diced pimentos, drained
8-oz can tomato sauce
1 tsp dried oregano
1 Tbsp red wine vinegar

Soffrito comes from the Spanish verb meaning "to sauté." Spanish soffrito is a sauce made by sautéing annatto seeds in rendered pork fat–this recipe is the Italian version. This thick tomato-bell pepper salsa is also a staple in Cuban kitchens. Use it to accompany chicken and rice dishes, Basque-style cod dishes, and omelets, or spread on tortillas for fajitas.

italian soffrito salsa

In a large pan over low heat, sauté the onions, green bell pepper, and garlic in the olive oil for about 15 minutes, until tender and lightly browned.

Add the pimentos and cook for 5 more minutes over low heat. Add the tomato sauce, oregano, and vinegar and cook for 10 more minutes.

Let cool, then store in a tightly closed jar in the refrigerator up to two weeks.

Serves 4–6

In this recipe, which originates from the exotic islands of the West Indies and Caribbean, the shrimp are marinated in a spicy vinaigrette, which gives them their punch. They can be marinated overnight, which makes this a perfect make-ahead dish for a party. All you need to do on the day is toast the pita! The result is a healthy, colorful, and flavor-rich dish.

island shrimp pita canapes

Ingredients

¼ cup cider vinegar
⅓ cup vegetable oil
½ Tbsp sugar
1 tsp Worcestershire sauce
¼ tsp hot-pepper sauce
½ tsp English-style dry mustard
1 tsp peeled and minced fresh ginger root
salt and freshly ground black pepper
8 oz medium shrimp, shelled and deveined
⅛ cup thinly sliced red bell pepper
⅛ cup thinly sliced yellow bell pepper
⅛ cup thinly sliced green bell pepper
⅛ cup cilantro, finely chopped
dried hot red pepper flakes (optional)
4 large, or 8 small, pita pockets, cut into about 12 wedges and toasted lightly
cilantro sprigs for garnish

In a saucepan, whisk together the vinegar, oil, sugar, Worcestershire sauce, hot-pepper sauce, mustard, ginger root, and salt and pepper to taste. Bring the mixture to a boil and simmer it, stirring occasionally, for 5 minutes.

Add the shrimp and simmer, stirring occasionally, for 3–5 minutes, or until they are cooked through.

Transfer the mixture to a heatproof bowl and add the bell peppers, tossing the mixture well. Chill, covered, for at least 2 hours, or overnight.

Drain the mixture, discarding the liquid, and stir in the cilantro, red pepper flakes if using, and salt and pepper to taste. Arrange the shrimp and several bell pepper strips on pita wedges. Garnish with cilantro sprigs.

Serves 4–6

Almost any thinly sliced smoked fish can be substituted for the Caribbean kingfish–just make certain skin and bones have been removed. Choose the plumpest shrimp, however, so that the treasure inside the "blanket" can be fully savored. A garnish of fresh dill and cherry tomatoes will add even more drama to the serving plate.

dilled shrimp in smoked kingfish blanket

Ingredients

- 2 Tbsp fresh lime or lemon juice
- ½ tsp salt
- 1 Tbsp chopped fresh cilantro
- ⅓ cup olive oil
- 1 Tbsp chopped fresh dill
- white ground pepper
- 24 cooked shrimp, shelled and deveined
- 4 oz smoked kingfish, thinly sliced and chilled
- fresh dill sprigs for garnish (optional)
- cherry tomatoes for garnish (optional)

Combine the lime or lemon juice, salt, cilantro, olive oil, dill, and pepper in a glass bowl. Add the shrimp, cover, and marinate for 2 hours.

Cut each slice of fish lengthwise into strips ¼ inch wide.

Wind a fish strip around each shrimp and fasten with a toothpick. Garnish and serve.

Ingredients

1-2 lb large raw shrimp with heads
coarse salt
about ¼ cup fat capers

For real mayonnaise
1 Tbsp white-wine vinegar
pinch of salt
2 large yolks (plus 1 egg white in a blender)
1¼ cups olive oil or 3:1 plain oil and extra virgin olive oil
freshly ground black pepper

Serves 4

Mayonnaise and fresh shrimp make perfect partners, and it is always worth making your own mayonnaise, which is infinitely superior to shop-bought versions. This classic recipe is easy to make.

fresh shrimp with caper mayonnaise

Make the mayonnaise. Put the vinegar and salt in a bowl (or blender or food processor). Add the egg yolks to the bowl (use 1 whole egg plus 1 yolk in a blender) and beat (or blend) to a cream.

Add the oil (not extra virgin) drop by drop, if working with a beater, until the mixture emulsifies. Add more oil in larger quantities as the mayonnaise thickens, until it is all absorbed. Add the extra virgin oil last, if using. Taste and correct the seasonings.

The mayonnaise can be thinned with 1½–3 tablespoons of boiling water if it is to be kept.

Cook the shellfish in a large pan of salted water. Large scampi with heads on (where 10–12 of them weigh 2 lb) will need about 6 minutes. Big deep-water shrimp need about 3 minutes and smaller shrimp 2 minutes. Cook little shrimp in batches—just plunging them in and out for a minute. Drain and serve in a big dish, scattered with coarse salt.

Crush the capers with the back of a spoon, stir into the mayonnaise, and pile into a bowl. Provide plates for the shells, and napkins, if the shellfish are still hot.

mussel, shrimp, and squid tapa

Serves 4

Tapas are an integral part of the Spanish lifestyle. This seafood tapa is light and tasty, and irresistibly easy to make. Tapas can be served either on their own as appetizers, or many tapas can be served together at the same time to make a meal.

Ingredients

- 7½ cups olive oil
- 1 lb shrimp in shell, frozen
- 3¾ cups lemon juice
- 2 lb mussels, cleaned, debearded, and any open ones discarded
- 1 lb squid, cleaned and blanched
- 3 tsp minced garlic
- 3 tsp paprika
- salt and freshly ground black pepper

In a saucepan, bring the oil to a boil and add the shrimp. Cover and take off the heat. Leave for 3 minutes to heat the shrimp through.

Add the rest of the ingredients, return to heat, and bring to a boil. Cover and shake until the mussels open.

Season to taste and serve in small bowls.

Serves 4

Try this mouth-watering dip with artichokes, lobster, scallops, crab claws, stone crabs, or any of your favorite fish dishes.

Ingredients

- ½ tsp salt
- 1 garlic clove, minced
- 1 small hot pepper, seeded and minced
- 4–5 Tbsp freshly squeezed lime juice
- 1 small onion, minced
- 6 Tbsp cold water
- 1–2 Tbsp minced fresh cilantro (optional)

Mash the salt with the garlic and hot pepper to form a paste. Stir in the lime juice, onion, water, and the cilantro if used. Let stand for 1 hour before serving.

Right: Mussel, shrimp, and squid tapa

Serves 4

These spicy croquettes are the snack of first choice from the Florida Keys to Miami.

Ingredients

1 lb conch, abalone, or squid, blanched and finely ground in a meat grinder or food processor
2 sweet green bell peppers, seeded and finely sliced
2 small onions, finely diced
2 tsp baking powder
3 celery stalks, finely chopped
1 large egg
2 tsp chopped fresh cilantro
½ tsp cayenne pepper
2 tsp Worcestershire sauce
1 garlic clove, minced
pinch of ground thyme
¼ tsp freshly ground black pepper
pinch of baking soda
1 cup milk
1¼ cups self-rising flour
vegetable oil

Mix together the conch (or substitute), bell peppers, onions, baking powder, celery, egg, cilantro, cayenne, Worcestershire sauce, garlic, thyme, black pepper, baking soda, and milk.

Slowly stir in the flour, then cover and refrigerate overnight.

In a deep, heavy saucepan or deep fryer, heat 2–3 inches of oil to 350°F.

Drop soupspoonfuls of the mix into the oil without crowding the pan. If the fritters bob to the top of the oil, submerge with tongs or a slotted spoon.

Remove from the oil when golden-brown on all sides. Drain on absorbent paper towels and serve immediately.

Serves 4

In Spain scallops have always been identified with St. James, and scallop shells are still the badge of pilgrims to his shrine. Galician scallops are huge, with creamy orange roes and big white muscles. Tomatoes and brandy make a splendid sauce for them.

st james's baked scallops

Heat the butter and 1 tablespoon of oil, and quickly fry the scallops for 2 minutes on each side. Shelled or defrosted scallops make a lot of liquid, so remove them when cooked, then boil this off.

Warm the brandy in a ladle, flame it, and pour it over the scallops. Spoon them into the upper shells or small heatproof dishes.

Add another 2 tablespoons of oil to the pan and fry the onion gently, adding the garlic as it softens. Add the chopped tomatoes, paprika, and cayenne pepper, and cook until the tomato has reduced to a sauce. Moisten with the wine or fish stock, add salt and pepper to taste, and spoon over the scallops.

Mix the bread crumbs and parsley and sprinkle thinly over the top of the scallops. Heat through for 2–3 minutes under the broiler at low heat, and serve immediately.

Cook's Tip

In Galicia the scallops are cooked in the curved upper shell. Ask for these at the fishmerchant (or use small dishes). To clean fresh scallops, hold a knife flat against the shell and cut the flesh free, then remove the ring of gristle round the white. Pull away any dark gut at the root of the coral.

Ingredients

14 oz shelled scallops (preferably 2–3 big ones on the shell per person)
1 Tbsp butter
3 Tbsp oil
4 Tbsp brandy
1 onion, finely chopped
3 garlic cloves, minced
7 oz ripe tomatoes, skinned and seeded (or use canned tomatoes)
1 tsp paprika
pinch of cayenne pepper
½ cup dry white wine or fish stock
salt and freshly ground black pepper
2–3 Tbsp fine bread crumbs
1 Tbsp chopped fresh parsley

Serves 4

Serve these tempting tidbits at your next party.

shrimp-chorizo fajitas in lettuce

Ingredients

8 oz chorizo, casing removed and finely diced
½ sweet green bell pepper, seeded and diced
½ sweet red bell pepper, seeded and diced
1½ tsp olive oil
8 oz medium raw shrimp, shelled, deveined, and diced
20 radicchio leaves
20 stuffed green olives for garnish (optional)

In a large skillet over medium heat, sauté the sausage and bell peppers in the oil for about 8 minutes, until the bell peppers are tender.

Stir in the shrimp and sauté for 2 more minutes or until the shrimp are no longer translucent.

Spoon about 2 Tbsp of the shrimp-chorizo mixture into each radicchio leaf. Roll each leaf and fasten it with an olive-studded toothpick.

Serve at once.

Serves 4

An extremely popular *tapa* in the Basque country of Spain, the name in Spanish, which means they are "wearing gaberdines," dates from the time that the Bonapartist army marched down from France in their waterproof capes. The lightest, crispest of batter coatings keeps the shrimp moist in the hot oil.

basque overcoated shrimp

Ingredients

1 lb large shrimp, in the shell
olive oil for deep frying
1 lemon, cut into wedges

For deep-frying batter
1 cup all-purpose flour
pinch of salt
¼ cup oil or melted butter
¾ cup tepid water
pinch of cayenne pepper
1 large egg white

Make the batter. Put the flour and salt in a blender (or bowl), work in the oil or butter, and then the warm water to make a smooth batter. Add a little cayenne. Let this stand while you peel the shrimp.

Heat the deep-frying oil (to top heat on an electric fryer). Beat the egg white until it forms soft peaks and fold it into the batter.

Dip each shrimp into the batter and drop into the oil. Let them puff up and color for about 30 seconds, then remove with a slotted spoon onto paper towels. Serve at once with the lemon wedges.

Serves 6

For this recipe, you need six large skewers and six healthy appetites!

monkfish skewers

INGREDIENTS

2 lb monkfish tail, skinned, boned, and cubed; marinate in liquid (3 parts water to 1 part lime juice)
½ large cucumber
1 red onion
lime wedges
tabasco sauce to taste

FOR SAUCE
4 red chiles, seeded and chopped
olive oil
2 large tomatoes, peeled and chopped
1 tsp oregano
1 tsp freshly ground black pepper
1 tsp cumin seeds
1 tsp ground ginger
2 tsp minced garlic
2½ cups fish stock

In a skillet, fry the chile in a little olive oil, until it becomes dark.

Blend together the chopped tomato, oregano, black pepper, cumin seeds, ginger, garlic, and fish stock. Add to the chiles. Bring the mixture to a boil and simmer for 10 minutes. Remove from heat.

Cut the cucumber into ¼-inch rounds. Cut the red onion into eighths, by halving like an orange, then quartering each half.

Make up the skewers. Pierce a piece of onion, a piece of fish, a piece of cucumber, etc., until the skewer is full. Coat liberally with the sauce.

Serve with lime wedges and tabasco sauce.

Serves 4

Another delicious seafood tapa, which originates from the Spanish town of San Sebastian in the mountainous Basque region.

anchovy and mussels san sebastian

Heat the olive oil in a skillet and gently fry the onions and bell pepper. Add the garlic and paprika, stir, and add the fish.

Simmer for approximately 5 minutes, then pour on the wine, vinegar, and stock. Bring to a boil.

Add the mussels, cover, and cook, until the mussels open.

Season to taste and serve in shallow dishes.

Ingredients

½ cup olive oil
2 medium onions, chopped
2 sweet green bell peppers, deseeded and finely chopped
1 tsp minced garlic
1 Tbsp paprika
1 lb anchovies, fresh, or 1 lb whitebait, frozen, defrosted
1 cup dry white wine
1 cup vinegar
1¼ cups fish stock
2 lb mussels, cleaned and debearded
salt and freshly ground black pepper

Makes 1–1½ cups

Use this pungent sauce as you would any other tomato-based salsa–with chips, over eggs, on tacos, or with meat.

garlic salsa

Ingredients

3 large tomatoes, peeled, seeded, and diced
½ cup chopped onion
1 jalapeño chile, trimmed of all but a few seeds and veins
¼–½ tsp salt
12 garlic cloves, minced
1 Tbsp chopped fresh basil or 1 tsp dried

Simmer the tomatoes, onion, jalapeño chile, and ¼ tsp salt for about 10 minutes to evaporate excess liquid.

Add the garlic and basil, and cook for another 2–3 minutes. Taste and adjust the salt if necessary.

Makes about 2 cups

This hot, smoky salsa gets its marvelous flavor from dried chipotle chiles. It is excellent with chips, on Huevos Rancheros (page 48), tacos, or with meat.

chipotle salsa

Ingredients

4 dried chipotle chiles
2 cups seeded and chopped tomatoes
½ cup chopped onion
½ cup chopped bell pepper
salt to taste

Remove the seeds and stems from the chiles, put them in a small, heat-proof bowl, and pour ⅔ cup boiling water over them. Let them soak for about 30 minutes, until they are pliable. If the chiles are very dry and brittle, gently simmer them in the water. Remove the stems, then put the chiles and the soaking water in a food processor. Purée.

Put the chipotle purée in a small saucepan with all the remaining ingredients. Simmer for 15–20 minutes, until any excess liquid evaporates. If the chipotles did not purée easily, or if you want a smooth sauce for dipping, briefly process the salsa again.

Cook's Tip

You may also use chipotle chiles canned in adobo sauce. Skip the steeping in hot water. Coarsely chop the chipotles before adding them to the salsa, then process after the salsa is cooked. Without the soaking water, there will not be as much excess liquid, and the salsa will not have to cook so long.

Makes 1–1½ cups

This is an all-purpose salsa, good with chips, over tacos and tostadas, with meat and fish, or mixed into rice.

basic salsa

Ingredients

4 medium tomatoes, cored and halved
1 cup chopped onion
5 serrano chiles, partly seeded if desired, minced
2 garlic cloves, minced
3 Tbsp chopped fresh cilantro
2 Tbsp fresh lime juice
1 Tbsp olive oil
¼–½ tsp salt

Cut the tomatoes in half and squeeze out the seeds. Broil the tomatoes, cut side down, on a broiler-safe baking sheet until the skins are partly blackened and slip off easily. Remove from the heat. Let them cool in a colander so that excess liquids drain off. Remove the skins.

Purée in a blender or food processor, but do not purée so long that the tomato becomes liquefied.

Stir together all the remaining ingredients and add the tomatoes. Let sit for 30 minutes, then taste and adjust the seasoning.

Makes about 2 cups

This easy recipe uses canned refried beans as a base, then adds spices, cheese, and Salsa Cruda to make it a flavorful dip. Serve it hot, with thick chips for dipping.

hot bean dip

Ingredients

- 1½ cups canned refried beans
- 1½ cups Salsa Cruda
- 1½ cups grated Cheddar or Jack cheese
- ¼ tsp ground cumin
- ¼ tsp dried oregano
- salt to taste
- ¼ cup sliced black olives
- 2 Tbsp chopped green onions

Heat the beans in a pan until they begin to bubble. Add the salsa, 1 cup cheese, the cumin, and oregano. Stir until the cheese has melted, then taste and add salt if needed.

Spoon into a heat-proof serving dish and garnish with the remaining cheese, the olives, and green onions.

Cook's Tip

If desired, garnish first with cheese only. Put the bowl in a 350°F oven for a few minutes until the cheese is melted, then garnish with the olives and green onions.

soups and snacks

Serves 4

albondigas soup

"Albondigas" is Spanish for meatballs, and traditionally, there are plenty of them in this soup–the recipe calls for generous portions of meat.

Ingredients

8 cups beef stock
1 small onion, chopped
2 tomatoes, chopped
1 medium potato, diced
1 medium carrot, sliced
1 zucchini, sliced
large pinch of oregano
salt and freshly ground black pepper

Meatballs

2 slices stale bread
4 oz ham or bacon
1 lb minced pork or veal (or half and half)
pinch of finely grated lemon zest
1 Tbsp lemon juice
pinch of dried thyme
½ tsp salt
pinch of cayenne pepper
2 large eggs
6–7 Tbsp flour
6–7 Tbsp olive oil

Crumble the bread by hand or in a food processor, and process (or chop) the ham or bacon. Mix in all the meat, lemon zest and juice, thyme, salt, and cayenne pepper. Combine with the eggs to make a rather wet mixture. Put spoonfuls of the mixture on a floured baking tray and roll to coat them with flour.

Fry the meatballs in the hot oil, shaking the pan to and fro every now and then, so they roll over and color to a good gold on the outside and are cooked through. They take about 10 minutes.

Combine the remaining ingredients and bring to a boil. Carefully insert the meatballs, which should be about the size of a golf ball or a little smaller, one by one into the soup. Simmer for at least an hour.

Serves 4

The orange in this soup brings out the sweet-acidic flavor of homegrown beefsteak tomatoes, if you are lucky enough to have some. Serve with jerk croûtons for an extra treat for the taste buds.

tomato-orange soup

Combine the tomatoes, basil, orange peel, green onion, sugar, and lime or lemon juice in a medium saucepan. Cover and bring to a boil. Lower the heat immediately and simmer, covered, for 15 minutes. Remove the orange peel.

Purée the mixture in a blender or food processor, and strain, if desired, to discard any seeds.

Return the liquid to the saucepan. Stir together the orange juice and cornstarch in a small bowl until smooth. Stir into the tomato mixture.

Cook over medium heat, stirring constantly, until the mixture thickens and comes to a boil. Lower the heat, stir in the cilantro, chives, or parsley, and salt and pepper to taste. Garnish with jerk croûtons, if desired.

Ingredients

2¼ lb ripe tomatoes, blanched, peeled and quartered (or canned whole tomatoes, undrained)
½ cup firmly packed fresh basil leaves
3 x ½-inch strips orange peel
2 Tbsp chopped green onion (white part only)
1 tsp sugar
2 Tbsp lime or lemon juice
1 cup orange juice
1 Tbsp cornstarch
2 Tbsp minced cilantro, chives, or parsley
salt and freshly ground black pepper
jerk croûtons (optional)

Serves 4

This tropical dish is an exciting fruity, spicy, mixture of flavors, in the best Creole tradition. It's rich, thick, and satisfying.

pineapple-mango bisque

In a small saucepan, combine the sugar, rum, and water. Bring to a boil over high heat and boil for 1–2 minutes, until reduced slightly. Remove from the heat and set aside to cool.

In a blender or food processor, combine the pineapple, mangoes, and rum syrup with ½ cup milk. Purée until smooth.

Strain the soup through a coarse strainer set over a large non-reactive bowl. Whisk in the remaining milk, the cinnamon, and the cream. Cover and refrigerate for at least 4 hours and preferably overnight. Serve well chilled.

Ingredients

3 Tbsp sugar
2 Tbsp dark rum
2 Tbsp water
3 lb pineapple, peeled, cored, and cut into 1-inch pieces
2 mangoes, peeled, pitted, and cut into ½-inch pieces
3 cups cold milk
pinch of cinnamon
½ cup chilled heavy cream, plus more for serving

Serves 6

INGREDIENTS

4 Tbsp butter
1 medium onion, finely chopped
1 fat garlic clove, crushed
6 oz fresh breadfruit, peeled, cored, and chopped
2½ cups chicken stock
1¼ cups light cream
1 tsp salt
¼ tsp freshly ground black pepper
2 tsp finely chopped fresh parsley

Serve this unusual soup chilled as a refreshing appetizer for a summer dinner party.

breadfruit soup

Melt the butter in a large saucepan. Add the onion and garlic and cook for 5 minutes, stirring, until they are soft but not browned.

Add the breadfruit and chicken stock and bring to a boil. Reduce the heat and gently simmer for 20 minutes, or until the breadfruit is tender.

Put half the mixture in a blender, along with half of the cream, and blend them together. Tip the purée into a bowl. Repeat for the remainder of the mixture, using the remainder of the cream. Season the creamy purée with the salt and pepper. Chill the soup, and sprinkle with chopped parsley before serving.

Serves 6

INGREDIENTS

2 onions
1 garlic clove
2 bay leaves
1 celery stalk, chopped
1 leek, chopped
1 tsp whole black peppercorns
1 Tbsp finely chopped fresh basil
1 tsp cumin seeds
1 tsp salt
5 cups cold water
1 lb whole fish (sea bream, red snapper, or mullet), cleaned and scaled
4 oz salt beef, diced
2 whole cloves
1 fresh hot pepper, sliced
1¼ cups coconut milk
3 Tbsp cornmeal
8 oz unshelled shrimp
1 Tbsp finely chopped fresh basil for garnish

Perfectionists may like to make coconut milk from the dried, grated flesh of whole coconuts. Canned coconut milk is a perfectly acceptable alternative.

fish and coconut soup

Slice one of the onions, and put the slices in a saucepan with the garlic, bay leaves, celery, leek, peppercorns, basil, cumin seeds, and 1 teaspoon salt. Pour in the 5 cups cold water.

Bring to a boil over moderate heat, then lower the heat, cover, and simmer for 15 minutes.

Add the fish and cook for 10–15 minutes, until the fish flakes easily when tested with a fork. Remove the pan from the heat, and then strain the stock into a clean pan. Reserve the fish.

Finely chop the second onion and add it to the fish stock, together with the diced beef, cloves, hot pepper, and coconut milk.

Bring to a boil over moderate heat, then lower the heat, cover, and simmer for 45 minutes, until the beef is tender, removing the hot pepper 15 minutes into this time and discarding it.

Sprinkle the cornmeal over the stock mixture and cook for 2 minutes, stirring constantly.

Skin and bone the fish, and cut the flesh into 1-inch pieces. Add the fish and shrimp to the soup, and cook over low heat for 5 minutes.

Serve in warmed soup bowls, garnished with the chopped, fresh basil.

Right: Breadfruit soup

Serves 4–6

Pumpkin makes a soup as tasty as it is colorful. In this recipe, the addition of coconut makes for a great symphony of flavors.

Put the pumpkin in a saucepan and add enough water (about 3¾ cups) to cover, together with 1 teaspoon of salt. Bring to a boil, then lower the heat and simmer for 20 minutes. Drain and reserve the cooking liquid.

Melt the butter in a clean saucepan over moderate heat. Add the onion and green onions and fry them, stirring constantly, for 5 minutes, until they are soft and golden.

Add the pumpkin, tomatoes, coconut milk, 3 cups of the pumpkin cooking liquid, half the nutmeg, a pinch of cayenne pepper, and salt and freshly ground black pepper. Bring to a boil, then lower the heat, cover, and simmer for 30 minutes.

Remove the pan from the heat and leave it to cool slightly. Purée half the soup at a time in a blender, then return it to the pan. Heat it through for 5 minutes, then pour the soup into warmed soup bowls and swirl a little of the sour cream or yogurt on top. Sprinkle with the remaining nutmeg, and serve at once.

Ingredients

2 lb pumpkin, peeled, seeded, and cut into 1-inch cubes
salt and freshly ground black pepper
2 Tbsp butter
1 large onion, finely chopped
3 green onions, trimmed and finely chopped
3 tomatoes, skinned and chopped
1 cup coconut milk
¼ tsp freshly grated nutmeg
pinch of cayenne pepper
⅔ cup sour cream or yogurt

Serves 4–6

The secret of this refreshing concoction is the seltzer and the extracts, which enhance the flavors of the tropical fruits. Serve in small soup bowls set in larger bowls lined with crushed ice–or serve in frosted glass mugs.

In a blender or food processor, purée the mango, star fruit, and pineapple until smooth. With the motor running, add the soda, apricot nectar or juice, lime juice, and pineapple extract. Process until blended. Cover and chill until ready to serve.
Float a star fruit slice in each serving and garnish with mint leaves, if desired.

Ingredients

1 small mango, peeled and cut into chunks
3 star fruit, 2 cut into small pieces and 1 sliced for garnish
⅛ medium pineapple, peeled
½ cup lemon-lime soda
6 Tbsp apricot nectar or juice
2 tsp freshly squeezed lime juice
1 tsp pineapple extract
fresh mint leaves for garnish (optional)

Left: Pumpkin soup

Serves 6

This icy, vinegar soup, made creamy with bread and oil, probably dates back to the Romans. Bell peppers and tomatoes were added after Columbus's voyage.

icy red gazpacho soup

Ingredients

2 slices stale white bread, crusts removed
1 small onion, chopped
2 garlic cloves, minced
2 Tbsp olive oil
1 tsp coarse salt
1 cucumber, seeded and chopped, with some skin removed
1 large red bell pepper, seeded and roughly chopped
4–5 big ripe red tomatoes, skinned and seeded
2 Tbsp red wine or sherry vinegar
scant 3 cups ice water
pinch of cayenne pepper

For Garnishes

4 Tbsp fried croûtons
2 hard-cooked eggs, peeled and chopped
4 Tbsp chopped bell pepper (red, green, or both)
4 Tbsp chopped onion or green onion
green or black olives, pitted and chopped

Soak the bread in water, then squeeze out. Put it in a blender or food processor with the onion, garlic, olive oil and salt, and purée.

Add the cucumber to the blender or food processor with the bell pepper. Then add the tomatoes and vinegar (you may have to do this in two batches in a small machine). Chill for at least 12 hours, preferably overnight, or freeze for about 30 minutes.

To serve, dilute with ice water (no ice cubes) and season to taste with the cayenne pepper.

Arrange the garnishes in little dishes and pass them around on a tray for everyone to help themselves.

Serves 4

Spiny fish, like *cabracho*, that swim round rocks are the basis of this rather elegant soup. It is made for the summer visitors, who flock to the seaside at Santander in northern Spain.

clams and leeks with pink santander soup

Simmer the fish with 1 onion, the bay leaf, a pinch of salt, the water, and half the wine for about 20 minutes. Strain, saving the stock. Remove the skin, bones, and head from the fish and flake the flesh.

Meanwhile, soften the second onion in the oil in a saucepan. Add the garlic and chopped tomatoes. Chop most of the leeks and add to the saucepan. Cook all this down to a sauce, stirring occasionally, then blend or press through a vegetable mill.

Put the purée in a casserole with the fish stock and the remaining wine. Bring to a simmer, add the rice, and cook for about 20 minutes, until tender. Add the remaining leek, sliced into strips, and the clams, about 5 minutes before the rice is cooked. When the clams open, give the casserole a good stir, and add the fish pieces. Season with salt and pepper to taste, and garnish with the egg.

Ingredients

1 whole fish, about 14 oz (*cabracho*, snapper), cleaned
¾ lb firm white fish (monkfish, conger, or cod)
2 onions, chopped separately
1 bay leaf
salt
4¼ cups water
⅔ cup dry white wine
3 Tbsp olive oil
1 garlic clove, minced
4 ripe tomatoes (skinned and seeded if using a blender), chopped
2 leeks, washed
½ cup rice
7 oz clams
freshly ground black pepper
1 hard-cooked egg, chopped

Serves 4

Chestnuts replace beans in the cooking of Galicia in Spain. They go into the paprika juices of fried sausages or around roast pork or duck. Here they make a delicious, creamy winter soup, flavored with cinnamon.

creamy chestnut soup

Slash the chestnut shells across the fat part of the nut, drop them into a pan, and cover with cold water with a little salt. Bring to a boil and cook for 20 minutes.

Let them cool (but leave under water). When they are cool, peel the chestnuts, removing any brown skin too.

Fry the bread in the oil, then purée in a blender or food processor with vinegar.

Reserve a handful of coarse nuts (chopped) to add texture to the soup and add the rest to the blender, a little at a time, with some of the stock. Purée to a cream.

Return the creamed soup to the pan, add remaining stock, taste, and season with salt and pepper. Flavor discretely with the cinnamon. Add the chopped nuts, heat through, and serve.

Ingredients

1 lb chestnuts unshelled or 12 oz peeled
1 thick slice bread
⅓ cup olive oil
3 Tbsp red wine vinegar
scant 3 cups light stock
salt and freshly ground black pepper
⅛ tsp powdered cinnamon

crab and greens soup

Serves 6

The leaves of dasheen, a tuberous plant also known as taro, called callaloo leaves in the Caribbean, give this tasty soup its other name, Callaloo.

INGREDIENTS

- ½ lb dasheen leaves or 1 lb fresh spinach
- 2½ Tbsp butter
- 1 onion, finely chopped
- 2 garlic cloves, crushed
- 1 fresh hot pepper, seeded and finely chopped
- 4 oz okra, trimmed and sliced
- 1 sprig fresh thyme
- 3¾ cups chicken stock
- 1¼ cups coconut milk
- salt and freshly ground black pepper
- 8 oz crabmeat, fresh, canned or frozen
- dash of hot pepper sauce

Wash the dasheen or spinach leaves, drain, and then shred them.

Heat the butter in a large saucepan over a medium heat. Add the onion and garlic and cook for 5 minutes, stirring occasionally until soft and golden. Add the hot pepper, okra, and thyme, and cook for 5 more minutes, stirring constantly.

Stir in the dasheen or spinach leaves and cook for 3 minutes, turning them in the pan to make sure that they are evenly cooked.

Pour the stock and coconut milk over the leaves, season with salt and freshly ground black pepper, and bring to a boil. Lower the heat, cover the pan, and simmer for 30 minutes.

Add the crabmeat, and cook for 5 more minutes, until it has heated through. Taste and adjust the seasoning if necessary. Stir in the pepper sauce and serve.

This soup has a hint of anis, although a big glass of dry white wine can replace the spirits. The initial part of the recipe also makes a good fish sauce or a tortilla filling.

catalan mussel soup

Clean the mussels. Cover them with cold water then scrub them one by one. Pull off all the "beards." Throw out any that are smashed or do not shut when touched.

Meanwhile, heat the oil in a casserole big enough to contain all the ingredients. Fry the onion gently, adding the garlic when it softens. Add the chopped tomato flesh and juice to the pan, and cook until reduced to a sauce. Add ⅔ cup of water to the pan.

Add the mussels in 2–3 batches. Cook with the lid on for 3–4 minutes, until they are open. Then use a slotted spoon to remove them to a plate and discard the top shell of each one. Throw away any that smell really strong or that remain obstinately shut. When they are all done, return them to the pan and sprinkle with the anis or Pernod.

Add more water—about 1½ cups—and bring back to a simmer. Season with salt and pepper, adding cayenne, and lemon juice to taste and parsley. Break a slice of bread into the bottom of each bowl and then ladle in the soup on top.

Ingredients

2 lb mussels
3 Tbsp olive oil
1 mild Spanish onion, chopped
1 garlic clove, minced
2 big, ripe tomatoes, skinned, seeded, and chopped
½ cup anis or Pernod
salt and freshly ground black pepper
pinch of cayenne pepper
juice of ½ lemon
3 Tbsp chopped fresh parsley
4 slices stale bread

Serves 4

Eggs appear on all Spanish menus, and shrimp are a popular addition, too. This is an economical way to eat them. Turnip leaves are the favorite green accompaniment, but you could use spinach or kale.

scrambled eggs with shrimp & spring leaves

INGREDIENTS

9 oz young turnip leaves or spinach, washed, trimmed and torn into small pieces
2 Tbsp butter
4 oz peeled shrimp
8 large eggs
2 Tbsp milk
salt and freshly ground black pepper
2 Tbsp olive oil

Blanch the young leaves in boiling water– just plunging them in and out– drain well, then chop them.

Heat the butter in 2 frying pans until it is frothing. Divide the leaves between them. Add the shrimp and heat through (cook for 2 minutes if they are raw).

Beat the eggs with the milk and seasoning. Add the oil to the pans, turn the heat to medium-high and pour the eggs over everything, scrambling them lightly and stirring the outside to the middle with a wooden spoon. Divide the contents of each pan between 2 plates, and serve accompanied with crusty bread.

This warming dish of spicy beans was made famous by a Madrid bar-keeper in the nineteenth century. In fact, he actually invented the recipe in the south of Spain, and the spicing is Arabic.

Serves 6

Madrid-style mildly spiced beans

Fry the onions gently in the olive oil in a casserole. Halfway through, add the pork or ham, and the garlic. Drain the beans and add them to the pot with the remaining ingredients and sufficient water to cover them well.

Simmer for about 1¼ hours, until the beans are soft, checking occasionally that they are not catching or drying out. There should be enough liquid left to give each person a couple of spoonfuls with the beans. Check the seasonings and serve in soup plates.

INGREDIENTS

- 1 lb dried haricot beans, soaked overnight
- 2 large onions, chopped
- 3 Tbsp olive oil
- scant 1 cup finely diced pork belly or ham
- 1 garlic bulb, cloves peeled and minced
- 3 Tbsp tomato paste
- 1 bay leaf
- 2 tsp paprika
- 1 Tbsp vinegar
- ¼ tsp ground cumin
- pinch of ground cloves
- 1 Tbsp chopped fresh parsley
- ¼ tsp white pepper
- 1 tsp salt

Serves 4

INGREDIENTS

1 large loaf French bread
4 level Tbsp mustard
1 lb smoked ham, thinly sliced
1 lb roast pork, thinly sliced
8 oz Swiss cheese, cut into narrow ¼-inch strips
tomatoes, thinly sliced
pickled dill cucumbers, thinly sliced
½ head Iceberg lettuce, shredded

This is one of south Florida's most popular snacks. Add some salami to the cold cuts, if you like. When it comes to the meats in this sandwich, the more the merrier.

sandwiches nuevo cubano

Slice the loaf in half lengthwise and spread both halves with mustard. Layer with alternating slices of ham, pork, and cheese.

Place both halves under the broiler until the unfilled half is slightly toasted. Add tomatoes, pickled cucumbers, and lettuce to the half with the meat and cheese on it. Top with other half and cut into 4 sandwiches.

Serves 4

Make this simple dish of baked tomatoes and ham extra special by adding ¼ cup of *fino* sherry and serving over green beans.

baked tomatoes with ham and egg

Preheat the oven to 350°F. Slice off the tomato tops and keep to one side. Excavate the tomatoes, salt the insides, and turn them upside down for 10 minutes.

Season the insides of the tomatoes with pepper and thyme, stuff with chopped ham or diced bacon, and then break an egg into each one.

Cover with the tomato tops again (to stop the yolks going hard). Bake in an oiled dish in the oven for 20 minutes.

Ingredients

4 large tomatoes
salt and freshly ground black pepper
pinch of thyme
good ½ cup chopped raw ham, or ⅓ cup diced, fried bacon
4–8 large eggs
oil for greasing

Cook's Tip

A ½ lb tomato will hold one eggs; a ¾ lb tomato will hold two eggs.

Serves 6 as a starter

Galician mussels are the best in the world, and this simple recipe shows them off perfectly. The thin pancakes are similar to the ones made in Brittany, which shares the same Celtic culture.

Wash the mussels, discarding any that are open (or you cannot close). Pull off beards.

Put the wine, onion, parsley stalks, and peppercorns into a pan and simmer.

Put in the mussels (in 2 batches) and cover. Cook over high heat for 3–4 minutes. Shake occasionally, until open. Discard the shells and any that remain shut or smell strongly. Strain the liquid into a measuring jug and leave to cool. Taste for seasoning.

Put flour into a bowl or blender and work in eggs, mussel liquor, and 3 tablespoons of cream. (Don't overbeat.) Let stand 1 hour.

Melt 1½ tablespoons of butter in a skillet, swirling it around. Add to the batter and stir thoroughly. Heat another ½ tablespoon of butter and swirl. Use about ⅓ of a cup of batter per pancake—pouring from a cup.

Lift skillet. Pour batter fast into middle and around skillet, tilting to cover the base.

Put the skillet back over the heat, shaking it to make sure the pancake does not stick. Cook for a minute until golden underneath, then flip over with a spatula. Briefly fry the other side. Roll and keep warm on a plate while you make more.

Warm the remaining cream in a saucepan with the mussel bodies. Spoon mussels and a little cream onto one edge of a pancake, sprinkle with parsley, and roll up. Serve immediately.

Ingredients

4 lb mussels
½ cup dry white wine
3 Tbsp chopped onion
4 parsley stalks, bruised
6 black peppercorns, crushed

Pancakes
scant 1 cup all-purpose flour
2 large eggs
mussel liquor (see method)
⅓–½ cup thick cream
5 Tbsp butter
½ cup chopped fresh parsley

Makes 16–24

Popular Mexican snacks, tamales are made from masa harina like corn tortillas, and filled with a variety of fillings. Deceptively simple-looking, tamales are surprisingly difficult to make–they fall apart, stick to the corn husks in which they are steamed, and generally misbehave. But they are worth the effort!

Ingredients

Dough

1 lb masa harina
1¼ cups of stock

Filling

3 California chiles
1 ancho chile
1 lb well-cooked beef, pork or chicken
4-6 cloves garlic

Variations

Variations in the dough include adding 1 cup of cream to the stock used to make it, and adding ¼ teaspoon each of cumin and oregano plus one puréed, soaked dried chile to the basic dough recipe.

Variations in the filling include using tomatoes, onions, and herbs such as rosemary, thyme, oregano and cumin.

Mix 1 lb of masa harina with the stock. Beat them until you have a light, soft, slightly mushy dough. A spoonful of the dough should float in water.

If you are using dried corn husks, soak them in hot water to soften them; this takes 30–60 minutes. Shake the water from the corn husks. Put 1 tablespoon of dough in the center of each husk, spreading it out until it is about ½ inch thick. Use your fingers or (much easier) a tortilla press.

Prepare the chiles. While they are soaking, shred the meat with two forks.

Liquidize the chiles in a blender with the garlic and a little of the soaking broth. Fry the purée for 5 minutes, stirring constantly, then add the shredded meat.

Put 1 tablespoon of filling in the center of the dough, then roll up the dough-plus-husk to enclose the filling, and fold the top and bottom of each husk over. Wrap another husk around and tie the ends with string.

Put the tamales in a steamer with the bottom end of the corn husk down. Steam for about 1 hour, or until the dough starts to come away from the husks.

Makes 1

Another tasty tapas dish from Spain, which teams well with crusty bread and olives, or with other tapas dishes. Light, nutritious, and easy to make.

tortilla española

Wash the potatoes, and peel them if you wish. Slice very finely and place in a pan of cold salted water. Bring to a boil and cook for 5 minutes (parboil). If preferred, the potatoes for this dish can be sautéed.

Place a skillet on the heat, add the oil and get it very hot. Add the onion very carefully, as the oil might spit. Toss.

Add the potato slices. Shake the pan, and stir to prevent them from sticking to the bottom. Season lightly with salt and pepper.

In a bowl, beat the eggs and season well. Lower the heat slightly, and cook the potatoes and onions, tossing until golden.

Tip the potato and onion into the egg mix, and mix well.

Replace the pan on the heat and, when it is hot, pour the mixture into it. It will seal immediately. Cook for 2 minutes, then turn the tortilla either by slipping it into another hot pan brushed with oil by placing pan no. 2 over pan no. 1 and flipping it, or by placing a large plate over the tortilla and turning it out onto the plate. Push the tortilla off the plate, back into the pan so that the uncooked side is now over the heat. Serve immediately.

Cook's Tip

When frying, if you find that the mixture becomes a little too dry, try adding more oil.

Ingredients

3 potatoes (or an equal amount of potato to onion)
3 Tbsp olive oil
1 onion, finely chopped or sliced
salt and freshly ground black pepper
3 eggs

Serves 4

Sardines are inexpensive, but flavorful. The sauce that accompanies them in this tapas dish enhances their flavor perfectly.

fried sardines

Ingredients

12 sardines (about 4 inches long)
½ cup seasoned all-purpose flour

For Marinade
2 tsp parsley, chopped
4 Tbsp lemon juice
½ tsp minced garlic
salt and freshly ground black pepper
4 Tbsp olive oil

For Sauce
salt and freshly ground black pepper to taste
1 large tomato, skinned and chopped
2 Tbsp chopped onion
enough mayonnaise to bind

First, make the marinade by blending all the ingredients together. Take the sardines (if the heads are on, leave them) and cut through the bellies lengthwise, without cutting through the bone. Butterfly the fish.

Paint the marinade on the fish, and leave for 20 minutes.

Shake the flour over the fish, dusting until well covered. Shake off any excess flour. Season.

Heat the oil until hot and fry the sardines, turning to brown both sides.

Prepare the sauce. Mix all the ingredients together, then either spoon it onto plates with the sardines, or use it as a dip.

Serves 4

Straight vegetable tapas are always in demand to accompany their meat and fish cousins. The mixture of seasonings in this recipe brings the beans alive.

green beans tapa

Place the beans in a pan of boiling salted water and cook for 6–8 minutes, until the beans are fairly firm but not raw. Drain well.

Melt the butter in a pan, add the olive oil, and heat. Add the onion and cook gently for 3–4 minutes.

Add the beans, salt and pepper, and toss. Add the chicken stock and the garlic.

Cover and cook for about 10 minutes, until tender. Season well and serve.

Ingredients

1 lb green beans, topped and tailed
½ stick butter
¼ cup olive oil
½ medium onion, finely sliced
salt and freshly ground black pepper
1¼ cups chicken stock
1 Tbsp minced garlic

Ingredients

For each quesadilla, you will need:

- vegetable oil or lard
- 1 flour tortilla
- ⅓ cup grated cheese or 2 4-inch squares of sliced Cheddar, Jack, or Mexican string cheese
- salsa to serve

Serves 4–6

Quesadillas show up in all kinds of restaurants with a variety of fillings–goat cheese, smoked chicken, lobster, and just about anything else imaginable. True Mexican quesadillas, however, are cheese empanadas–turnovers made with fresh corn tortilla *masa* (dough).

Very lightly oil a heavy skillet that is at least as large as the tortilla (usually about 8 inches in diameter). You need only enough oil to season the tortilla and keep it from sticking. Heat the skillet, then place the tortilla in it, making sure it lies flat. Reduce the heat to low.

Place the cheese on one half of the tortilla, and fold the other half over the cheese. Lightly brush the top of the folded tortilla with oil. As the cheese begins to melt and the quesadilla holds together, carefully turn it over. Cook until the cheese has completely melted and the tortilla has a few brown spots.

Remove from the heat, cut into wedges, and serve with salsa for dipping.

Instead of folding the tortilla, you can double the amount of cheese and make a sandwich with a second tortilla. This method is faster if you're cooking quesadillas for a large number of people.

For variety, add any combination of the following to the cheese filling: strips of roast poblano or jalapeño chiles, or sweet red bell pepper; chopped green onions; chopped cilantro; mushrooms sautéed in butter and garlic; cooked meat, such as grilled chicken, smoked sausage, beef or pork: cooked seafood, such as shrimp or crab; and black bean salsa.

The following items are best cold, rather than cooked in the quesadilla, so serve them over the top, or pry open the cooked quesadilla and put them inside: black olives; sliced avocado; chopped fresh tomatoes; and sour cream (on top or as a dip).

Cook's Tip

Quesadillas are typically served with a tomato salsa, but don't overlook the possibilities of a tomatillo salsa, black bean salsa, or avocado salsa. Or use two salsas–one type in the filling, and another for dipping. If you're feeling really bold, try a fruit salsa with a meat or fish filling.

Serves 4

INGREDIENTS

1–1½ cups salsa of your choice
oil for frying
4 corn tortillas
4 eggs
1 cup grated Cheddar cheese
chopped green onions and cilantro for garnish

Huevos Rancheros is a traditional Mexican breakfast dish, with as many variations as there are families. This is a simple version made with tortillas, fried eggs, cheese, and salsa. Any tomato or tomatillo salsa is suitable, or try a black bean.

huevos rancheros

COOK'S TIP

For a heartier breakfast, fry 2 eggs per serving. Since this dish is made in steps, use heatproof plates, and keep them warm in the oven between steps.

Preheat the oven to 150°F and put the plates in to warm. Warm the salsa in a small saucepan over low heat.

Heat a little oil in a skillet. Fry the tortillas, one at a time, for a few seconds per side, just enough to soften. Drain each tortilla and put them on a plate in the oven.

Discard all but 1 tablespoon of oil. Keep the heat at medium. Break the eggs onto saucers, and slide them into the hot oil. Cook for 2–3 minutes, until the yolks are set, spooning hot oil over the top of the eggs or covering the pan to keep the heat in. If desired, turn the eggs and cook for about 30 seconds longer.

Put 1 egg on each tortilla. Top with salsa and sprinkle the cheese over the top. Garnish with green onions and cilantro.

meat dishes

Serves 6

In this Brazilian-inspired dish, a leg of lamb is marinated, then roasted or grilled, and served with salsa. It is a relatively simple dish that requires a minimum of last-minute work.

lamb with black bean salsa

Ingredients

leg of lamb, about 5 lb
⅓ cup olive oil
¼ cup red wine vinegar
2 Tbsp fresh orange juice
4 garlic cloves, minced
1 tsp dried oregano
½ tsp dried rosemary
⅓ cup finely chopped onion
1½ cups Black Bean Salsa or Black Bean-Papaya Salsa

Cook's Tip

Weight is for bone-in meat. If you plan to grill the lamb, ask the butcher to remove the bone and butterfly the meat so that it lies relatively flat.

Put the lamb in a non-metallic dish. First make the marinade; combine all the remaining ingredients except the salsa and then pour the marinade over the lamb, making sure that the entire surface is coated. Marinate the lamb in the refrigerator for at least 2 hours and up to 24 hours, turning it occasionally and at the same time spooning marinade over it.

Roast the lamb in a 350°F oven or over a barbeque. Lamb is cooked rare when it reaches an internal temperature of 140°F (test with a meat thermometer—about 20 minutes per pound in the oven, considerably less time on a barbecue. Lamb is traditionally served rare or medium rare (about 150°F). It is easier to carve if it is allowed to rest for about 20 minutes after it comes out of the oven. Serve with the salsa.

Serves 4

Serve the sauce over the chicken and accompany with cooked vegetables and pasta or rice.

honey-rum chicken with mushroom sauce

Use a sharp pointed knife to make several holes in the chicken breasts. Mix the orange juice and honey, and marinate the chicken in it for 20 minutes.

In a large, heavy-based skillet, brown the chicken in 1 tablespoon of clarified butter. Remove from the heat and set aside.

Melt the remaining butter in the same skillet, then add the garlic and mushrooms, and sauté for 1 minute. Pour in the rum and flame it. Add the chicken stock, salt and pepper, and chicken, and simmer over low heat for 30 minutes.

Just before serving, beat the cream with the eggs and add to the skillet. Cook over low heat for about 1 minute. Add the cilantro, check the seasoning, and cook for a further 1 minute. Garnish with orange slices, if desired, and serve.

Ingredients

4 large chicken breasts, boned, skinned, and fat cut off
¼ cup orange juice
1 Tbsp honey
1½ Tbsp clarified butter
2 garlic cloves, minced
1 cup sliced button mushrooms
1 cup sliced oyster mushrooms
1 cup dark rum
2 cups chicken stock
salt and freshly ground black pepper
½ cup light cream
2 eggs, beaten
2 Tbsp chopped fresh cilantro
orange slices for garnish (optional)

Serves 4–6

This is an elegantly simple dish. It is rather rich, and so is ideal as part of a long-drawn-out *comida*, where each course is fairly small. A large serving might be overwhelming!

chicken cilantro

Chop the onion and garlic, and fry them together in the olive oil and/or butter until the onion is tender and transparent.

Cut the chicken into cubes about 1 inch on a side. Fry with the onions and garlic until the chicken is cooked through—this should take no more than 5–10 minutes, depending on the temperature and the size of the cubed chicken. The meat should be browned slightly on the outside, but only in places. Add the chopped cilantro leaves, stir for a few seconds to coat, and serve.

The pan juices are the usual sauce, but for a much stronger-flavored (and darker-colored) sauce, deglaze the pan with half a glass of dry white wine or vermouth.

Serve with plain boiled rice.

Ingredients

- 1 small onion
- at least 1 garlic clove
- 4 Tbsp olive oil or butter (or a mixture of the two)
- 4 small, boned, skinless chicken breasts
- 2 Tbsp chopped cilantro leaves
- salt and freshly ground black pepper

Serves 4–6

A classic Creole dish, Trinidad-style stewed chicken is a unique way of cooking chicken, combining a tantalizing medley of tastes.

trinidad-style stewed chicken

Ingredients

- 2 Tbsp lime juice
- 1 medium onion, chopped
- 1 large tomato, cut into 8 wedges
- 1 celery stalk, chopped
- 1 Tbsp chopped green onion
- 3 Tbsp minced fresh cilantro
- 1 garlic clove, minced
- ⅛ tsp dried thyme, crumbled
- 1 tsp salt
- ⅛ tsp freshly ground black pepper
- 1 Tbsp white wine vinegar
- 2 Tbsp Worcestershire sauce
- 1½–2lb chicken, cut into serving pieces
- 2 Tbsp vegetable oil
- 2 Tbsp firmly packed dark brown sugar
- 2 Tbsp tomato ketchup
- 1 cup water
- 2 cups shredded cabbage (optional)
- celery leaves for garnish (optional)
- lime slice for garnish (optional)

In a large bowl, combine the lime juice, onion, tomato, celery, green onion, cilantro, garlic, thyme, salt, pepper, vinegar, and Worcestershire sauce. Add the chicken, turning it to coat well, and leave it to marinate in the refrigerator, covered, overnight.

In a heavy kettle, heat the oil over medium-high heat until it is hot but not smoking, and add the sugar. When the sugar mixture begins to bubble, transfer the chicken in batches to the kettle, using a slotted spoon. Reserve the marinade mixture.

Cook the chicken, turning it until it is browned well, and transfer it to paper towels to drain.

Stir the reserved marinade mixture, ketchup, and water into the fat remaining in the kettle and return the chicken to the kettle. Bring the mixture to a boil and simmer it, covered, stirring occasionally, for 30 minutes.

Add the shredded cabbage, if using, and simmer for 15–20 minutes, until the thickest pieces of chicken are done. Garnish with celery leaves or lime slices if wished.

Serves 4

The original "duck with orange" comes from the city that introduced bitter oranges to Europe in the eleventh century. Their juice and the olives make the duck seem fatless. Since it is a party dish, an elegant modern presentation is given here.

duck with oranges and olives, seville style

INGREDIENTS

1 oven-ready duck (preferably gray barbary)
salt and freshly ground black pepper
3 Tbsp olive oil
1 onion, finely chopped
1 sweet green bell pepper, seeded, and chopped
1 large tomato, skinned, seeded, and chopped
1 Tbsp all-purpose flour
¾ cup dry sherry
1 Seville orange (or 1 sweet orange plus ½ lemon)
1 bay leaf
8–10 parsley stalks, bruised
¾–1¼ cups duck stock from giblets (or chicken stock)
2 large winter carrots
1¼ cups green olives, rinsed

Quarter the duck, removing the backbone, visible fat, and hanging skin. Season and prick the remaining skin well. Heat the oil in a small casserole and brown the duck on all sides.

Remove the duck and all but 3 tablespoons of fat from the casserole. Fry the onion in this fat until soft, adding the bell pepper and tomato halfway through. Sprinkle with the flour and stir in. Add the sherry and stir until simmering.

Fit the duck pieces back into a casserole compactly, tucking in the backbone and 2 strips of thinly pared orange zest. Slice the orange (and lemon, if using)—do not peel it—and tuck these around the duck, pushing in the bay leaf and parsley stalks. Add enough stock to almost cover, and simmer, with the lid on, for 45 minutes.

Quarter the carrots lengthwise, remove the cores, and cut them into olive-sized lengths. Round the corners with a knife to make oval shapes, then simmer them in boiling water for 5 minutes.

Remove the duck pieces and discard the backbone, parsley stalks, orange strips, and bay leaf. Purée the sauce through a vegetable mill, rather than a blender, which will give too smooth a sauce. Return the duck to the casserole and pour in the sauce.

Add the olives and carrot shapes and simmer for another 10 minutes until the carrots are tender.

Move the duck pieces to a serving dish with a slotted spoon. Surround the meat with the carrots and olives and keep warm. If there is too much sauce, boil to reduce it a little. Any floating fat can be removed by pulling strips of paper towels across the surface. Check the seasoning, pour the sauce over the duck, and serve.

Serves 8

Pozole, a long-simmering pork and hominy stew, is a traditional dish that dates back many centuries with Mexicans and native Americans of the Southwest. This version of pozole is a main dish, but you can omit the cubed pork and serve it as a side dish or appetizer, if you prefer.

INGREDIENTS

¾ cup chopped onion
4 Tbsp vegetable oil
3 garlic cloves, minced
2 quarts chicken stock
1 lb pork neck bones
2 ancho chiles
2 dried California chiles
3 Tbsp all-purpose flour
1 tsp salt
1 tsp dried mustard
2 tsp dried oregano
2 tsp ground cumin
½ tsp cayenne pepper
½ tsp freshly ground black pepper
3 lb pork roast or other pork cut, cut into bite-sized cubes
4 cups canned hominy
2 to 3 cups Cucumber Salsa or Salsa Cruda

In a large casserole, sauté the onion in 1 tablespoon of oil for 5 minutes. Add the garlic and cook for 1 minute longer, then add the chicken stock and neck bones. Note the level of the liquid, then add 2 cups water. If the stock falls below that level during cooking, add more water. Bring the stew to a boil, reduce the heat, and simmer, uncovered, for 2 hours.

While the stew is simmering, cut the dried chiles in half and remove the seeds. Put the chiles in a small, heat-resistant bowl and pour ½ cup boiling water over them. Let soak for 20 minutes, stirring once or twice to be sure all parts of the chiles are softened. Purée the water and chiles in a blender, then add this purée to the simmering stew.

After the stew has simmered for 2 hours, remove it from the heat. Remove the pork bones. If you have time, let the stock and the bones cool for ease of handling. Skim the fat from the stock and return the stock to the stove. Take off any meat from the bones and add it to the stew. Discard the bones and fat.

Mix together the flour, salt, mustard, oregano, cumin, cayenne, and black pepper. Toss the pork cubes in this seasoning mixture until evenly coated.

Heat the remaining oil in a large skillet and sauté the pork just until it is golden-brown. Add the pork cubes to the stew, bring to a boil, then reduce the heat and simmer, covered, for 20 minutes. Add the hominy and simmer for 10 minutes longer.

Taste the stock and adjust the salt to taste. Ladle the pozole into large bowls and serve with Cucumber Salsa or Salsa Cruda.

Serves 8

This traditional dish from northeastern Spain is an early example of what has recently come to be known as "surf and turf."

catalan pork with mussels

Heat the fat in a wide casserole, season the pork well, and fry until it is golden on all sides. Remove from the pan.

Add the oil and chopped onions and cook gently until soft. Add the garlic, tomatoes (breaking them up with a spoon), paprika, chile or cayenne, bay leaves, and orange peel or zest, and cook for 20 minutes until reduced.

Meanwhile, open the mussels in a big saucepan. Put in the wine and 3 tablespoons of parsley. Add half the shellfish and cover tightly. Steam for 4 minutes, shaking the pan occasionally if they are not all in one layer. Remove the first batch of mussels from the pan and proceed to cook the second batch.

Remove the top shells from each mussel and throw away any mussels that smell strongly or that remain obstinately shut.

Add the pork and the mussel liquor to the sauce and simmer for 30 minutes, until the meat is tender and the sauce has reduced. Check the seasoning, add the mussels, and warm through. Sprinkle generously with parsley and serve.

Ingredients

- 1¾ lb lean pork, cubed
- salt and freshly ground black pepper
- 3 Tbsp rendered fat or lard
- 3 Tbsp olive oil
- 1½ lb onions, chopped
- 6 garlic cloves, minced
- 2 x 14-oz cans tomatoes
- 1 Tbsp paprika
- ½ dried chile, seeded and chopped, or a pinch of cayenne pepper
- 2 bay leaves
- 1 strip of dried orange peel or 2 strips of fresh zest
- 3 lb mussels, cleaned
- scant 1 cup dry white wine
- ½ cup chopped fresh parsley

Serves 8–10

This is a favorite dish in Puerto Rico, where it is known as *Fabada Asturiana*, and it perfectly demonstrates the Puerto Rican love of assertive, spicy flavors. Adjust the amount of onions and squash according to how many you wish to serve.

roast pork puerto rican-style

Ingredients

1 Tbsp minced garlic
3 Tbsp olive oil
½ tsp dried oregano, finely crumbled
¾ tsp ground cumin
1 tsp salt
½ tsp freshly ground black pepper
1 cup chopped green onions
1 cup chopped fresh cilantro
1 cup chopped sweet green bell pepper
1 cup white rum
1 leg of pork (about 7 lb) with bone)
2 x 8-oz baking potatoes, scrubbed, each cut lengthwise into 8 wedges
1–3 large red onions, each cut into 8
2–4 pieces squash, such as Hubbard or butternut, or calabaza, peeled and cut into 1-inch slices (optional)
2–3 yellow summer squash or zucchini cut into 1-inch slices (optional)

For Gravy

4 Tbsp fat from drippings in roasting pan
4 Tbsp all-purpose flour
4 cups water or beef stock

Sauté the garlic in the olive oil until tender. In a blender or food processor, blend the olive oil–garlic mixture with the oregano, cumin, salt, pepper, green onions, cilantro, green pepper, and rum to make a paste.

Place the meat in a non-reactive baking pan, which is slightly larger than the meat. With a long, sharp knife, score the top of the roast in a diamond pattern, cutting through the rind and underlying fat almost to the meat. Rub the seasoning paste into the roast, cover, and marinate in the refrigerator overnight.

Preheat the oven to 325°F. Unwrap the meat and roast it for 2 hours. Add the potatoes, onions, and squash, if using, to the roasting pan and brush with drippings. Roast for 1 hour, then add the summer squash, or zucchini, if using, and brush with drippings. Continue to roast for another 45 minutes (the meat should roast for a total of 32–35 minutes per pound or until a meat thermometer inserted in the thickest part (not touching the bone) registers 185°F and the vegetables are tender).

Remove the meat to a chopping board and cover loosely with foil (reserve the pan drippings for gravy). Let stand for 15 minutes before slicing. Arrange the vegetables on a platter and cover to ensure they keep warm.

If you are planning to reserve some of the meat and pan gravy for other meals, proceed as follows. Slice one third of the pork and serve it with the vegetables, reserving 1 cup of pan juices for gravy. Then slice half the remaining pork thinly (about 1 lb) and wrap tightly in heavy freezer wrap. Shred the remaining meat (about 12 oz), cover, and refrigerate. Sliced pork will keep for 2 weeks in the freezer; shredded pork for about 1 week in the refrigerator.

To make the gravy, pour the fat into a medium saucepan and sprinkle the flour into it. Whisk over medium-high heat until smooth, scraping up browned bits. Gradually whisk in the water or beef stock until blended. Bring to a boil, reduce the heat, and simmer for 5 minutes or until thickened, stirring 2 or 3 times. Cool and refrigerate about half the gravy in a tightly sealed container if you are planning to use it in another meal.

Serves 4

Manchamantel is a type of bright red, fruity sauce, used for simmering chicken and pork. Its name translates as "tablecloth stainer"–perhaps because of its lurid color, perhaps because in the enthusiasm of the moment, diners tend to spill a lot of the lovely sauce as they aim for their mouths.

pork in manchamantel sauce

Ingredients

2 ancho chiles
1 guajillo chile
2 cups hot water
½ onion, toasted
3 garlic cloves, toasted
4 tomatoes, toasted and lightly charred
1 cup meat or chicken stock, or ½–2 bouillon cube mixed with water
½ tsp ground cinnamon
⅛ tsp ground cloves
salt and freshly ground black pepper
1–2 Tbsp oil
1–2 Tbsp vinegar
1–2 tsp sugar
2 lb boneless pork, in serving pieces
1 zucchini or chayote, cut into bite-sized pieces
1 apple, preferably tart, peeled, cored, and diced
½ carrot, thinly sliced
dried fruit: several tablespoons raisins, several prunes, a dried pear, apple, and apricot (optional)
½ ripe pineapple, peeled and cut into bite-sized chunks
1 banana, diced

Cook's Tip

Manchamantel sauce can be prepared without the meat and used with foods grilled over coals: the richness of duck is especially nice with the fruity sauce.

Toast the chiles on an open flame until they turn color but do not blacken. Place them in a pan of hot water and simmer for 20 minutes, or until the chiles are softened.

Remove the stems and seeds and, in a blender or food processor, purée the chiles with enough of their soaking liquid to make a smooth purée.

Skin roast the onion and garlic, and dice them. Dice the tomatoes (leave on their charred skin—it adds flavor). Add the onion, garlic, and tomatoes to the chile purée, and whirl to make a smooth sauce. Season with cinnamon, cloves, and salt and pepper.

Heat the oil and when it is almost smoking pour in the sauce. Cook for a few minutes until it concentrates and darkens slightly, then add the vinegar, sugar, and pork.

Cook for about 1¼ hours, then add the zucchini or chayote, apple, carrot, dried fruit, if using, and pineapple. Continue to simmer until the fruit and meat are tender.

Adjust the seasoning and sugar-vinegar balance, then add the banana and warm through. Serve immediately.

Serves 6

Salt beef is a popular ingredient in the Caribbean–both in recipes and as an accompaniment to bread. This stew is hearty and satisfying.

Ingredients

- ½ lb lean salt beef
- ½ stick butter
- 1 Tbsp vegetable oil
- 2 lb boned lamb or goat, cut into 1-inch pieces
- 2 onions, finely chopped
- 1 large tomato, skinned and chopped
- 2 tsp peeled and chopped fresh ginger root
- ¼ sweet green bell pepper, chopped
- 1 fat garlic clove, minced
- ½ fresh hot pepper, chopped
- 1 tsp salt
- 2 tsp ground cumin
- 2 Tbsp lime or lemon juice
- 2½ cups water
- 3 potatoes, peeled and diced
- 2 cucumbers, peeled and diced

Put the salt beef in a saucepan, cover with cold water, bring to a boil, and boil for 30 minutes. Drain the meat and cut it into cubes.

Heat the butter and oil in a large saucepan, then add the lamb or goat and brown it all over. Remove the meat and set to one side.

Add the onions to the saucepan and cook for 5 minutes. Add the tomato, ginger, green bell pepper, garlic, hot pepper, salt, and cumin. Cook for 10 minutes, stirring constantly.

Stir in the prepared salt beef, lamb or goat, lime or lemon juice, and 2½ cups of water. Cook for 1 hour over low heat.

Add the potatoes and cucumber, and simmer for 20 more minutes.

Cook's Tip

Salt beef is cured in salt in the same way as salt pork. It may be blanched to extract excess salt.

Serves 4

Although it is sometimes made as a tapa, serve this dish with rice or pasta as a main meal. If you wish, add sliced mushrooms to increase the number of portions.

andalusian kidneys in sherry

Fry the onion in 3 tablespoons of oil over low heat in a big skillet. When it starts to soften, add the diced bacon or ham, and the garlic.

Remove the membranes and cut out the cores from the kidneys, then cut them into large dice. Remove and reserve the onion and bacon from the pan, and add 2–3 tablespoons more oil.

Put in the diced kidneys, a handful at a time, over the highest heat, and stir occasionally. When they are sealed, pull them to the sides of the skillet and add the next handful. When they are all sealed and colored, return the onions and bacon, sprinkle with flour, and stir in. Add the sherry, tomato paste, and thyme and bring to simmering point. Season to taste.

Ingredients

1 large onion, chopped
⅓ cup olive oil
4 oz bacon or ham, diced
1 garlic clove, minced
10 fresh lambs' kidneys
3 Tbsp flour
½ cup dry sherry
1 Tbsp tomato paste
2 sprigs fresh thyme
salt and black pepper

Serves 4–6

The literal translation of the Spanish is "old clothes" because that's how drab a pile of shredded beef looks. This dish looks great with some extra Soffrito (page 12), or try it tucked inside warmed flour tortillas, with a bowl of Soffrito on the table for spooning extra spiciness atop. A garnish of pimentos is highly recommended.

Place the steak in a large casserole and add water to cover completely. Add the halved onion, about half of the garlic, the celery, and salt, and bring to a boil. Cover, reduce the heat to moderate, and cook for about 1¼ hours, or until the meat is tender. Transfer the meat to a plate, let it cool, then cover, and refrigerate until chilled.

Shred the chilled meat with your fingers and set aside. If it doesn't shred easily, pound it between a layer of baking parchment, and it should easily pull apart.

In a large skillet, heat the olive oil. Add the remaining garlic and cook over high heat for about 1 minute, until lightly browned. Reduce the heat to moderate and stir in the sliced onion and bell pepper. Cook, continuing to stir occasionally, for about 10 minutes, until softened.

Stir in the tomatoes, wine or sherry, bay leaves, cumin, and a pinch of salt. Increase the heat to moderately high and cook, stirring occasionally, for about 25 minutes. Remove the bay leaves.

Add the shredded meat, stir, and cook for about 5 minutes, or until the meat is heated. Stir in the peas, if desired, and then remove from heat. Season to taste with salt and pepper. Garnish, if desired, with the canned pimentos, and serve immediately.

Ingredients

- 2 lb skirt or flank steak
- 1 large onion, halved
- 4 garlic cloves, minced
- 1 large celery stalk, chopped
- 1 Tbsp salt
- 1 large onion, thinly sliced
- 4 Tbsp olive oil
- 1 large sweet green bell pepper, deseeded and cut into thin strips
- 3 large ripe tomatoes, finely diced
- ½ cup dry white wine or 2 Tbsp dry sherry
- 2 bay leaves
- 2 Tbsp ground cumin
- 1 oz cooked mange-touts at room temperature (optional)
- salt and freshly ground black pepper
- 2 oz canned pimentos, drained and chopped for garnish (optional)

fried lamb with lemon juice

Serves 4

In some restaurants in old Castile (now modern Spain), whole lambs are baked in great domed ovens. At home, cuts of lamb are more likely to be fried simply with lemon juice. This is one of the nicest ways to cook fatless meat.

INGREDIENTS

- 1¾ lb trimmed tender lamb, in strips
- salt and freshly ground black pepper
- 3 Tbsp olive oil
- 1 onion, chopped
- 2 garlic cloves, minced
- 2 tsp paprika
- generous 1 cup stock or water
- juice of 1 lemon
- 3 Tbsp finely chopped parsley

Season the lamb with salt and pepper. Heat the oil in a casserole over your hottest burner and add the meat in handfuls.

Add the onion, and keep turning the meat around with a wooden spoon. Add more meat as each batch is sealed, with the garlic and more oil if necessary.

When the meat is golden and the onion is soft, sprinkle with paprika and add the stock or water. Continue to cook over medium heat until the liquid has virtually gone.

Sprinkle with the lemon juice and parsley, cover, and simmer for 5 minutes. Check the seasonings before serving.

rabbit with saffron and aromatics

Serves 4–5

Rabbit, highly spiced with thyme and cumin, was introduced to Spain by the Arabs nearly a millennium ago.

INGREDIENTS

- 2 large onions, chopped
- ⅔ cup olive oil
- 1 garlic clove, minced
- 30 saffron strands
- salt and freshly ground black pepper
- 2½ lb rabbit, in pieces
- generous 1 cup white wine
- 15 black peppercorns, lightly crushed
- ¼ tsp ground cumin
- 1 tsp paprika
- pinch of cayenne pepper
- 6 sprigs of thyme
- 1 bay leaf, crumbled

Fry the onions slowly in 3 tablespoons of oil in a skillet, adding the garlic as they soften. Powder the saffron strands in your fingers and soak in ⅓ cup of hot water.

Remove the onion and garlic from the pan and add about ⅓ cup more oil. Season the rabbit and fry the meaty portions (back legs and saddles) for 10 minutes. Tuck in the thinner pieces and fry for about another 10 minutes until everything is golden. Remove the rabbit and drain off all the oil.

Add the wine and stir to deglaze the pan. Pack the rabbit pieces tightly into a small casserole, and add the onion, wine, saffron liquid, crushed peppercorns, cumin, paprika, and cayenne. Tuck in the thyme and the crumbled bay leaf. Add ½ cup water to almost cover the meat.

Cover and simmer very gently for about 1 hour until tender, making sure it does not get dry. Taste and add more seasonings—be as bold as you dare; you are unlikely to season it more than the locals do!

Right: Rabbit with saffron and aromatics

INGREDIENTS

2 lb rabbit, chopped into 2-inch pieces
1 tsp salt
freshly ground black pepper
½ stick butter
1 medium onion, chopped
1 fat garlic clove, minced
2 Tbsp brandy
2 Tbsp sherry
3 ripe tomatoes, skinned and chopped
½ fresh hot pepper, chopped
⅓ cup canned drained pimentos, finely chopped
⅔ cup chicken stock
1 bay leaf
½ tsp sugar

If possible, use homemade chicken stock in this recipe. If you use a bouillon cube or granules, you may want to reduce the amount of salt used to season the rabbit pieces.

rabbit in pimento sauce

Preheat the oven to 350°F. Season the rabbit pieces with the salt and freshly ground black pepper to taste. Heat the butter in a large casserole dish and brown the rabbit. Transfer the meat to a dish and put to one side.

Add the onions and garlic to the casserole, cook them for 5 minutes, then pour them over the rabbit.

Pour the brandy into the casserole and heat it. Remove the casserole from the heat, and set light to the brandy with a match. Shake the casserole backward and forward until the flame dies. Add the sherry to the brandy in the casserole and bring to a boil. Add the tomatoes, hot pepper, pimentos, chicken stock, bay leaf, and sugar, and season to taste with freshly ground black pepper. Add the rabbit, bring to a boil, and cook for 30 minutes.

Remove the casserole from the heat, and cover. Bake in the preheated oven for about 2 hours.

Serve with rice.

fish and seafood

Serves 6

Ingredients

about 6 Tbsp olive oil
1 onion, chopped
2 garlic cloves, minced
5 cups fish stock
scant 1 cup dry white wine
40 saffron strands or large pinch of saffron powder
1 cup raw shelled shrimp
salt and freshly ground black pepper
pinch of cayenne pepper
6 chicken thighs or 3 legs, halved
1½ cups arborio rice
1 tsp paprika
2 cups cleaned mussels
1 cup cooked green beans or peas
7 oz canned red pimentos, drained
¼ cup chopped fresh parsley

This great star turn of the Valencian coast in eastern Spain has always been cooked outdoors. Preparing it takes all morning and it is cooked by the men, so the whole thing becomes a party. This more modest version needs a good stock and a suitably shallow, wide 13–14-inch paella pan.

Fry the onion in 3 tablespoons of oil in the paella pan, adding the garlic when it softens. Warm the stock and wine together, soaking the saffron in a cupful of it.

Meanwhile, start a second skillet, heating 3 tablespoons of oil. Fry the shelled shrimp for 2 minutes (omit this stage if they are already boiled), then reserve. Rub salt, pepper, and the cayenne into the chicken pieces and fry for about 10 minutes on each side, adding more oil if needed.

Wash the rice in a strainer and drain. Add the rice to the onion in the paella pan, stir for a couple of minutes and sprinkle with the paprika. Add the saffron liquid and one third of the stock and bring back to a boil. Set the kitchen timer for 20–25 minutes. When the liquid has been absorbed, add another third of the stock, and distribute the mussels, shrimp, and beans or peas round the pan.

When the liquid has nearly gone, add the remaining stock and give the mixture a last stir. Add the chicken pieces, bedding them into the liquid round the pan. Simmer on the lowest heat (ideally on a heat diffuser) for about 8–10 minutes. The liquid should all disappear by the time the timer rings. Check that the rice is cooked.

Cut the pimentos into strips and lay these across the rice. Then turn off the heat and wrap the paella pan in newspaper or foil, to keep in the steam.

Let it stand for 10 minutes. The flavors will blend and the last drop of liquid should disappear. Sprinkle with parsley and serve.

It speeds things up to prepare the base for the rice in the paella pan, and to use a second pan for frying the shellfish and chicken pieces.

Serves 2

Recipes from the Caribbean often utilize the rich fruits of the tropical sea, of which one of the kings is the lobster.

cuban lobster in chile sauce

Ingredients

2 x 2-lb uncooked lobsters, split in half lengthwise
2 Tbsp vegetable oil mixed with 1 tsp liquid annatto
1¼ cups dry white wine
1 tsp salt
½ hot pepper, finely chopped

Remove and discard the gelatinous sac in the head of each lobster and the long intestinal vein attached to it. Chop off the tail section of each lobster at the point where it joins the body. Twist off the claws, and smash the flat side of each claw with a large, heavy knife. Cut off and discard the small claws and antennae.

Heat the oil in a large skillet. Add the lobster bodies, tails, and large claws and fry them, stirring constantly, until the shells turn pink. Transfer the lobsters to a large plate.

Add the wine to the skillet, and bring it to a boil. Stir in the salt and hot pepper. Return the lobsters to the pan, coat them evenly in the liquid, and cook for 10 minutes, basting them from time to time.

To serve, arrange the lobster pieces in a large, heated dish and spoon the sauce over them generously.

Makes 1 pie

An empanada is a Spanish pie that can have a variety of fillings. It can be bound in a shortcrust, a bread dough, or even a puff pastry made with lard. Individual pies are sometimes made, although it is more usual to bake a large one in a paella pan and serve it cold in slices–a delicious centerpiece to any tapas display.

Ingredients

4 Tbsp olive oil
1 small onion, chopped
1 tsp minced garlic
2 sweet green bell peppers, deseeded and cut into fine strips
3 tomatoes, peeled and halved
2 red chiles, seeded and chopped
1 lb squid, cleaned and sliced into rings
1 cup red wine
1 cup fish stock
1–2 tsp salt
2 tsp paprika
sprig of fresh thyme
1 lb mussels, cleaned, debearded, and simmered in a little boiling salted water for 5 minutes
8 oz peeled shrimp
salt and freshly ground black pepper
2 tomatoes, sliced and peeled
1 egg yolk mixed with a little milk to glaze the pie

For Dough

2¼ cups all-purpose flour
generous ⅛ cup fresh yeast or 1/16 cup dried yeast
1⅛ cups tepid milk
½ stick butter
2 eggs
1 tsp salt

Prepare the filling. Heat the oil in a large skillet and gently cook the onion and garlic. Add the bell peppers and tomatoes. Add the chiles, stir, and cook for 10 minutes. Add the rings of squid, with the chopped legs.

Pour in the red wine and stock, cover, and cook for 20 minutes over moderate heat. Add the salt, paprika, and thyme, and stir. If the mixture looks a little dry, add some water.

Remove the mussels from the shells and add to the mixture along with the shrimp. Remove from the heat and season.

Make the dough. Sift the flour into a bowl and make a well in the center. Crumble or sprinkle the yeast into the well. Pour in the tepid milk and stir to dissolve the yeast. Cover with a fine layer of flour, but do not blend this in.

Cover the bowl with a cloth and leave the mixture to rise for 15 minutes in a warm place. When the yeast has risen enough, cracks in the covering layer of flour should begin to appear.

While the mixture is rising, melt the butter in a pan, add the eggs, and beat into the butter. Stir in the salt and cool slightly to blood temperature. Pour this egg and butter mixture over the floured yeast in the bowl. Stir with a wooden spoon and beat until the dough is thoroughly mixed.

Knead the dough, by stretching and pulling it with your hands until it is dry and smooth. If the dough is too soft, add a little more flour. Shape it into a ball, place in the bowl, and dust lightly with flour. Cover the bowl with a dish towel. Leave to rise in a warm place for 20 minutes. The dough should at least double in volume.

Knead through again and leave it to rise for a further 20 minutes, covered. It is now ready for use.

Grease and line a paella pan with half the dough. Add the filling, remembering that the pie will rise to fill the pan. Cover with the slices of tomato and a little salt.

Roll out the remaining dough, and place over the top, sealing the edges well. Glaze with the egg yolk and decorate as desired. Most Spanish cooks stick to a very simple pattern of thin crisscrossed strips. Leave to stand for 10 minutes before baking at 400°F for 30 minutes. Leave to cool and slice.

Serves 6

A gumbo is a Creole specialty that has become a mainstay of New Orleans cuisine. A thick, stew-like dish, it can have any of many ingredients, including several meats or shellfish such as sausage, ham, chicken, shrimp, oysters, or, as here, crab. Vegetable gumbos are also popular. Okra is used to thicken the mixture.

crab gumbo

Ingredients

- 2 x 2-lb cooked crabs
- 2 Tbsp butter
- 1 Tbsp vegetable oil
- 1 onion, chopped
- 1 x 14-oz can tomatoes, drained and chopped
- 1 Tbsp chopped fresh thyme
- 2 Tbsp chopped fresh parsley
- 8 oz okra, trimmed and sliced
- 1 fresh hot pepper
- 2½ cups boiling water
- salt and freshly ground black pepper

Cut the legs and claws off the crabs, and crack them using a nutcracker. Cut the body into quarters.

Heat the butter and oil in a large saucepan over medium heat. Add the onion and fry for 5 minutes.

Add the crabs and cook, turning over the pieces frequently.

Stir in the tomatoes, thyme, and parsley, and cook for 5 more minutes.

Add the okra and hot pepper, and pour in 2½ cups of boiling water. Season with salt and freshly ground black pepper, then lower the heat, and simmer for 45 minutes.

Discard the hot pepper, and spoon the stew into warmed soup bowls. Serve with fresh bread.

Serves 6

This Galician recipe is straightforward to make because it needs no fish stock. It is a good dish for using a mix of strange fish, but do not include mackerel or any oily fish.

mixed fish and shellfish stew

Ingredients

2¾ lb white fish, cleaned
6 Tbsp olive oil
1½ lb onions, chopped
1 lb clams, mussels, etc., cleaned
salt and freshly ground black pepper
1½ Tbsp paprika
10 black peppercorns, crushed
1 *guindilla* or ½ dried chile, seeded and chopped
freshly grated nutmeg
⅔–¾ cup chopped parsley
¾ lb shrimp
2 cups dry white wine

Cut off the spines and fins from the fish with scissors and remove all scales by stroking the fish from the tail to the head with the back of a knife or your thumbs. Rinse the fish inside and cut off the heads. Cut whole fish across into sections, 2 inches long, and cut the fillets into similar-sized pieces.

Warm 3 tablespoons of oil in the bottom of a deep, flameproof casserole. Put in a good bed of onions. On this arrange a layer of one third of the fish, choosing from the different varieties. Pack half the clams or mussels into all the spaces. Season with salt, ½ tablespoon of paprika, half the peppercorns, a little ground pepper, and *guindilla* or chile, and the nutmeg. Sprinkle with 1 tablespoon of oil and plenty of parsley. Make a layer of shrimp on top.

Repeat all the layers. Make a top layer of fish, seasoning as before and packing onion into the gaps. Add more parsley. Add the wine and about 1 scant cup of water to almost cover. Then re-season the top layer, adding ½ teaspoon of paprika and another tablespoon of oil.

Bring to simmering (the best part of 10 minutes), then cover, turn down the heat, and simmer for 15 minutes. Check the stock seasoning and lay a spoon, as well as a knife and fork on the table, so that everyone can taste it. Take the shrimp heads off before eating, if you wish.

Serves 4

If snapper is not available, substitute any firm-fleshed, lean fish, such as grouper, halibut, haddock, flounder, perch, talbot, or sole. Serve this with steamed vegetables; it goes especially well with cauliflower, or if you're feeling daring, try it with fried green plantains, which you can dip into the orange-curry sauce.

steamed red snapper with orange-curry sauce

Make the sauce. Combine the sour cream, orange rind, cilantro, onion powder, mustard, and curry powder in a small bowl, and chill.

Lightly grease a vegetable steaming rack and place it in a flameproof casserole. Add water to just below the steaming rack and bring it to a boil.

Toss the allspice berries into the boiling water and place the fish on the rack. Cover, reduce the heat, and simmer for 8–10 minutes or until the fish flakes easily when tested with a fork. Serve with the sauce.

Cook's Tip

There are about 250 varieties of snapper, red snapper being the most popular. Some varieties of rockfish are sold under the names "Pacific snapper" and "red snapper," and one variety of tilefish is sold under the name "yellow snapper"–none of these are true snappers, though.

Ingredients

3 whole allspice berries
1½ lb red snapper, cross-sectioned into 4 steaks

For Orange-curry Sauce
½ cup sour cream
4 Tbsp grated orange rind
2 Tbsp chopped fresh cilantro
¼ tsp onion powder
¼ tsp dry mustard
¼ tsp curry powder

Serves 4

Ingredients

- vegetable oil
- 1 medium onion, sliced
- 1 large tomato, peeled and chopped
- ½ tsp ground allspice
- ¼ tsp dried oregano
- ¼ tsp dried thyme
- 1 tsp chopped fresh cilantro, or to taste
- ½ bay leaf
- 2 Tbsp water
- 1 tsp hot pepper sauce
- 1 lb red snapper fillets
- ½ Tbsp lime or lemon juice
- 1 small garlic clove, minced
- ½ large onion, chopped
- ¼ red bell pepper, chopped
- ¼ sweet green bell pepper, chopped
- ½ Tbsp olive oil
- ¼ cup sliced almonds

You'll be surprised how the mélange of spices and tomatoes in this dish permeates the fish with West Indian flavors. Serve with fluffy rice to soak up some of the juices.

Preheat the oven to 400°F. Coat a 13 x 9 x 2-inch baking dish with vegetable oil. Arrange the sliced onion in the dish, and add the tomato, allspice, oregano, thyme, cilantro, and bay leaf. Combine the water and hot pepper sauce, and gently pour over the tomato mixture. Rub the fish fillets with lime or lemon juice and arrange in the dish.

Sauté the garlic, onion, and red and green bell peppers in olive oil for about 3 minutes. Spoon over the fish.

Cover and bake in the oven for 40–45 minutes or until the fish flakes easily when tested with a fork. Remove the bay leaf and garnish with the almonds.

> **Cook's Tip**
>
> You can substitute any firm, white-fleshed fish such as perch, turbot, sole, grouper, halibut, haddock, or flounder for the snapper in this recipe.

Serves 6

Ingredients

- 6 small, boned flying fish
- 1 Tbsp lime or lemon juice
- 1 garlic clove, minced
- salt and freshly ground black pepper
- 1 tsp chopped fresh thyme
- 2 whole cloves
- 2 tsp all-purpose flour
- vegetable oil

This deliciously light and tasty dish originates from Barbados, where this white, slightly salty fish is plentiful.

Marinate the fish in the lime or lemon juice, garlic, salt and freshly ground black pepper, thyme, and cloves for at least 1 hour.

Remove the fish from the marinade, and dry them well with paper towels.

Mix the flour with freshly ground black pepper, then coat the fish in it, shaking off any excess.

Heat some oil (enough to cover the fish) in a large skillet. Fry the fish until they are golden-brown, then serve with rice and peas, salad, and hot pepper sauce.

Serves 4

Considered a delicacy even in Florida, pompano may be hard to find. Substitute any firm-fleshed, thin white fish or sea scallops.

lemon-scented pompano on spinach & leeks

In a steamer, combine the lemon, lime, bay leaves, and water. Cover and simmer over low heat for 2 minutes.

Bring the liquid to a boil over high heat. Spread sliced leeks, one layer thick, in a steamer basket. Cover and steam for about 3 minutes, until tender.

Uncover, pack in all the spinach or Swiss chard, re-cover and steam, stirring once, until wilted, which will take about 4 minutes. Transfer the steamer basket to the sink and press the vegetable mixture very lightly to extract excess moisture.

Transfer the vegetable mixture to a large skillet and set aside. Return the water with the lemon, lime, and bay leaves to a boil over high heat. Lay the fish fillets in the steamer basket, cover, and steam for 3–4 minutes, until the fish are just cooked through and flake easily if tested with the tip of knife. Quickly reheat the leek mixture over high heat, sprinkling soy sauce on top and tossing, for about 1 minute.

To serve, arrange the leek mixture and fish on warm plates. Season the fish with pepper to taste.

Ingredients

1 small lemon, thinly sliced
1 small lime, thinly sliced
6 bay leaves
1½ cups water
1 large leek, split, thinly sliced crosswise, and rinsed
1 lb spinach or Swiss chard, stems removed
½ lb pompano fillets
1 tsp mild soy sauce
freshly ground black pepper

Serves 4

Lime-marinated shrimp are sautéed, then cooked briefly in Chipotle Salsa (page 25), which imparts its hot, smoky flavor to the shrimp. Serve them on their own or over plain white rice.

shrimp in chipotle salsa

INGREDIENTS

- ⅓ cup olive oil
- ⅓ cup fresh lime juice
- 3 garlic cloves, minced
- 1¼ lb medium or large shrimp, peeled and deveined
- 1½ cups Chipotle Salsa
- ½ tsp salt

Mix together 2 tablespoons of olive oil, the lime juice, and the garlic to make a marinade. Put the shrimp in a glass or other non-reactive bowl. Pour the marinade over the shrimp, and toss so that all the pieces are coated. Let marinate for 30 minutes.

Heat the remaining oil in a large skillet. Remove the shrimp from the bowl, reserving the marinade. Add the shrimp to the oil and sauté quickly over medium heat for about 1½ minutes. Remove the shrimp. Set aside.

Add the salsa to the remaining oil and fry it, stirring almost constantly, for 5 minutes.

Add the marinade and salt, and cook for another 2 minutes. Return the shrimp to the skillet and cook for about 2 minutes longer, long enough to cook through the shrimp and let them absorb some of the salsa flavors.

Serves 4

If you are unable to find a fresh red snapper, try this dish with sole or sea bass instead. You could also use sea bream.

yucatan red snapper

INGREDIENTS

- 2 small bell peppers, one red, one green
- 1 medium onion, chopped
- 2 garlic cloves
- ½ stick butter
- 2 Tbsp chopped cilantro leaves
- 1 tsp whole cumin seeds
- ½ tsp grated orange rind
- ½ cup freshly-squeezed orange juice
- 1 red snapper, 4–5 lb, cleaned and scaled
- 6–8 sliced black olives
- salt and freshly ground black pepper
- 1 large or 2 small avocados for garnish

Preheat the oven to 325°F. Seed, devein, and chop the bell peppers. Chop the onion. Chop the garlic finely. Fry them all together in 2 tablespoons of butter, until softened. Add the cilantro, cumin, orange rind, and orange juice, and season to taste. Simmer for 2 minutes.

Thickly grease the bottom of a large, shallow, ovenproof casserole with the rest of the butter. Put the fish in the casserole and cover it with the sauce. Scatter the olives over the top.

Bake for about 30 minutes, basting occasionally with the sauce. Serve hot, garnished with thin slices of avocado.

Right: Shrimp in chipotle salsa

Serves 4

Here's a delicious shrimp dish with a quite unusual flavor, thanks to the tamarind it contains. Add a crisp salad and serve on steamed rice.

shrimp tamarindo

Ingredients

2 Tbsp butter
2 Tbsp minced onion
1 garlic clove, minced
1 sweet green bell pepper, cored, seeded, and chopped
2 Tbsp tomato paste
¼ cup sherry
1 bay leaf
½ cup tamarind juice
2 Tbsp clear honey
¼ tsp ground allspice
¼ tsp salt
⅛ tsp hot pepper sauce
1 lb medium shrimp, shelled and deveined
1 Tbsp fresh lime or lemon juice

Heat the butter in a large skillet. Add the onion, garlic, and bell pepper, and sauté until tender.

Add the tomato paste, sherry, bay leaf, tamarind juice, honey, allspice, and salt, stirring constantly until heated through.

Reduce the heat and simmer, uncovered, for about 5 minutes, until slightly thickened. Add hot pepper sauce to taste.

Add the shrimp and stir until pink, which will take 3–5 minutes. Remove the bay leaf and stir in the lime or lemon juice.

Serves 6

This Caribbean dish is as colorful as it is delicious. Lemon enhances the delicate taste of the fish and the bread crumbs add interesting texture.

cuban baked fish with onions

Clean, wash, and prepare the fish. Make an incision along the belly of each fish. Lightly sprinkle salt and freshly ground black pepper and some garlic both inside and outside. Rub lemon juice over the fish.

Place the fish in a pan, pour the water over the fish, and leave to marinate for at least 1 hour, preferably 4 hours.

Preheat the oven to 350°F. Cook half the onion, the remaining garlic, and half the bread crumbs in 1 tablespoon of the oil. Add a little water to make the mixture form a slightly crumbly texture, and leave it to cool.

Stuff the fish with the onion and bread crumb mixture, then lay them in a greased baking dish. Cover with the rest of the oil.

Sprinkle the rest of the onion and bread crumbs and the parsley over them, then bake in the oven for 30 minutes. Serve immediately.

Ingredients

- 2 lb red snapper or similar fish
- salt and freshly ground black pepper
- 2 garlic cloves, minced
- juice of 1 lemon
- 1 cup water
- 1 large onion, finely chopped
- 6 Tbsp fresh bread crumbs
- ½ cup olive oil
- 1 Tbsp chopped fresh parsley

Serves 4

There are trout in all the mountain rivers in Spain, and a favorite recipe is to cook the fish simply with mountain herbs and a fruity red wine.

trout in red wine

Ingredients

2 small trout, cleaned
1 small onion, chopped
6 black peppercorns, crushed
1 bay leaf, crumbled
2 sprigs of thyme
1 sprig of rosemary
4 parsley stalks, bruised
2 sprigs of mint, plus extra for garnish
scant 1 cup red wine
¼ cup olive oil
salt
½ Tbsp butter
½ Tbsp all-purpose flour
¼ cup chopped fresh parsley
baby potatoes to serve

Rinse the cleaned trout, dry them, and pack them into a baking dish. Sprinkle with the onion, black peppercorns, crumbled bay leaf, thyme, rosemary, parsley, and mint. Pour in the red wine and leave to marinate for at least 2 hours.

Preheat the oven to 375°F. Sprinkle the fish with the oil and a little salt and put the dish in the oven. Cook for 15 minutes for 9-ounce trout, 20 minutes if they are any larger.

Drain off the cooking liquid into a saucepan. Mash together the butter and flour, and drop it into the wine mixture to thicken it a little, stirring. Bring back to a simmer, then pour over the trout, and sprinkle with parsley.

Serve with new potatoes, cooked or garnished with fresh mint.

vegetable, salad, and side dishes

Serves 4

This simple vegetable dish is transformed by the use of Creole "jerk" seasoning, an exciting blend of herbs and spices. (For an example of jerk seasoning, see recipe for Jerk Mon's Chicken, page 52)

Ingredients

8 small new potatoes (about 1 lb), peeled (optional) and quartered
¾ tsp any dry jerk seasoning
1 Tbsp butter, melted
2 Tbsp chopped fresh cilantro
cilantro sprigs, for garnish (optional)

Place the potatoes in a steamer rack over boiling water. Cover and steam for 12–15 minutes or until tender.

Transfer the potatoes to a bowl and sprinkle with jerk seasoning. Add the butter and cilantro and toss to coat the potatoes thoroughly.

Garnish with cilantro sprigs, if desired. Serve with any fish or meat dish, or on its own as a snack.

Serves 4

Bring a taste of the tropics to your table in no time with this simple dish. It's wonderful with ham or pork chops, and with its bright color you won't need a garnish.

sweeter-than-sweet sweet potatoes

Ingredients

4 large sweet potatoes, boiled and sliced
2 x 8-oz cans crushed pineapple, drained
½ tsp grated nutmeg
2 tsp grated fresh ginger root
2 tsp ground cinnamon
2 Tbsp dark rum

Preheat the oven to 350°F. Layer the sweet potatoes in an ovenproof dish.

Combine the pineapple, nutmeg, ginger, cinnamon, and rum, and pour over the potatoes. Bake for 5 minutes and serve.

Serves 4

This dish offers a variety of tastes and textures, and couldn't be more colorful. For a very special occasion, garnish with the orange slices, pecans, and toasted coconut.

so-sweet sweet potatoes and carrots

In a vegetable steamer over boiling water, steam the carrots for 2 minutes. Add the sweet potatoes, cover, and steam for 8–10 minutes, until tender but not mushy. Set aside.

Drain the pineapple, reserving 1 cup of juice. Combine the juice, water, sugar, cornstarch, soy sauce, vinegar, zest, and salt in a saucepan. Place over medium heat and bring to a boil, stirring.

Add the pineapple and raisins, and simmer for 1 minute. Combine the vegetables and pineapple mixture in a large bowl and stir gently. Serve now or proceed to next step, if a garnish is desired.

Preheat the oven to 350°F. Line the sides of an 8-inch flameproof serving dish with overlapping oranges. Scoop the contents of the bowl into the dish and sprinkle the top with pecans and coconut. Place in the oven for 10 minutes or until the coconut browns.

Ingredients

12 oz carrots, sliced into 2-inch thick rounds
12 oz sweet potatoes, peeled and cubed
16-oz can unsweetened pineapple chunks, undrained
scant 4 Tbsp water
2 Tbsp brown sugar
1 Tbsp cornstarch, dissolved in 1 Tbsp cold water
2 tsp soy sauce
1 tsp vinegar
½ tsp grated orange zest
⅛ tsp salt
¼ cup golden raisins
2 seedless navel oranges, peeled and thinly sliced (optional)
½ cup pecan halves for garnish (optional)
2 tsp shredded coconut for garnish (optional)

Serves 4

INGREDIENTS

12 Anaheim or Poblano chiles
1 lb Cheddar or Jack cheese, cut into 12 pieces
1 cup all-purpose flour
6 eggs
vegetable oil for frying

This classic Mexican way of preparing *chiles rellenos* can be rather time-consuming to make if you use fresh chiles. On the other hand, canned chiles will not be anything like as good as fresh ones–use them only if you are desperate for time.

mexican stuffed hot peppers

Roast and skin the chiles. Slitting open the side of the chile, remove the seeds and veins, but be careful not to break the flesh. Into each chile, insert a piece of cheese "stuffing," tapering the end of the cheese slightly, if necessary. Roll the peeled, seeded, stuffed chiles in flour.

Beat the egg yolks and whites separately; the whites should be beaten to the stiff peak stage. Re-combine the eggs and beat together quickly.

Dip the chiles in the egg batter, making sure that you cover the whole surface evenly. Fry in fat or oil that is more than 1 inch deep. Keep them warm in the oven until you are ready to serve.

Serve with Refried Kidney Beans (page 90) and basic spiced rice.

Serves 4

INGREDIENTS

1½ cups boniato, grated
1½ cups evaporated milk
1 cup coconut milk
3 very ripe bananas, mashed
1 cup firmly packed brown sugar
1 egg
½ tsp ground cinnamon
½ tsp grated nutmeg
1 tsp vanilla extract
½ Tbsp dark rum
2 Tbsp unsalted butter, melted
grated rind of ½ lime

This aromatic Haitian dish is a sweet potato pudding using boniatos, the white-fleshed tropical tuber with a scent like that of violets. If you cannot find boniatos in your area, substitute ordinary white potatoes and add 1 teaspoon allspice to the dish.

Preheat the oven to 400°F. Mix together the boniato and evaporated milk, coconut milk, bananas, sugar, egg, spices, rum, butter, and lime rind.

Pour into a buttered baking dish and bake for about 1 hour. Serve warm or cool.

Right: Mexican stuffed hot peppers

Serves 4

This is an excellent accompaniment to meat tapas. The more often you refry the beans, the better they taste.

Place all the ingredients except the bacon and butter in a pan, bring to a boil, and simmer for 40 minutes.

Place one quarter of the total in a food processor and purée. Remix the puréed beans with the whole beans.

Chop the bacon and place it in boiling water for 10 minutes to remove the saltiness. Remove from the water and drain.

Heat the butter in a skillet and fry the bacon.

Add the beans, little by little, to the skillet and mash with the back of a spoon. Season well.

The beans should go into a thick purée. Season, sprinkle with parsley, and serve.

Ingredients

1-lb can kidney beans
1 red chile
1 medium onion
2 tsp minced garlic
1 tsp paprika
salt and freshly ground black pepper
5 cups water
6 slices good bacon, without the rind
½ stick butter
3 Tbsp chopped parsley

Serves 6

A Friday Lent dish in many Spanish households, this soup-stew is made with, or without, salt cod. The latter makes a pleasant vegetarian dish.

garbanzo beans with spinach

Remove the bones and skin from the salt cod (if using) and shred the flesh. Put the drained garbanzo beans, salt cod, the whole onion stuck with a clove, whole carrot, bay leaf, and parsley stalks into a big casserole and add 5 cups of water. Bring slowly to a simmer, skim off the bubbles, then cover and simmer for 1½–2 hours.

Heat the oil in a skillet and fry the chopped onion. As it softens, add the garlic, tomatoes, and paprika. Cook down to a sauce, seasoning with salt and pepper. Add the spinach to a saucepanful of boiling water—just in and out for young spinach, but cook older leaves for 2–3 minutes. Drain and chop.

When the garbanzo beans are almost tender, remove the bay leaf, parsley stalks, whole onion, and carrot. Discard the clove, and purée the onion and carrot in a blender or food processor with ¼ cup of the garbanzo beans and half a ladleful of their liquid. Check the overall amount of liquid—the garbanzo beans should barely be covered at this point.

Add the tomato sauce and onion purée to the casserole. Taste for seasoning—plenty is needed. Add the spinach, simmer for another 20 minutes or so to blend the flavors, then check that the garbanzo beans are tender. This dish is traditionally served with chopped hard-cooked egg on top.

Ingredients

7 oz salt cod, soaked overnight (optional)
1 cup garbanzo beans, soaked overnight
2 onions, 1 whole, peeled, 1 chopped
1 clove
1 large carrot
1 bay leaf
2–3 parsley stalks, bruised
¼ cup olive oil
2 garlic cloves, minced
2 ripe tomatoes, skinned and chopped
1 tsp paprika
salt and freshly ground black pepper
1¾ lb spinach, trimmed and washed
2 hard-cooked eggs, peeled and chopped

Serves 2

Serve this as a simple but good appetizer before meat, or by itself as a vegetarian supper dish. It is one of the few eggplant dishes that omits salting the flesh, so is quick to prepare.

navarre-style mushroom-stuffed eggplants

Ingredients

2 eggplants, about ¾ lb each
2 small onions, chopped
3 Tbsp olive oil
3 garlic cloves, finely chopped
2½ cups cleaned and sliced mushrooms, preferably including wild ones
salt and freshly ground black pepper
béchamel sauce
½ cup grated hard cheese

Halve the eggplants lengthwise and remove the flesh carefully, so that the skin is not broken. Reserve the skins and chop the flesh finely.

Fry the onions in the oil in a skillet until they color. Put in the garlic and mushrooms, and cook until they soften. Add the eggplant flesh and fry until golden, stirring occasionally. Season the eggplant skins and the flesh in the skillet, then stuff the skins with the fried mixture.

Pour a pool of béchamel sauce into a gratin dish. Arrange the stuffed vegetables on it, then dribble the remaining sauce into the eggplants. Sprinkle them with cheese, brown under a hot broiler for 5 minutes, and serve.

Serves 6

Eggplant dishes in the Mediterranean date from the time of the Moors. This one must have been updated when tomatoes, bell peppers, and potatoes were introduced from America. It is typical of the rather solid soups and vegetable dishes of the Balearic islands.

layered eggplant, potato, and tomato casserole

Preheat the oven to 400°F. Slice the eggplants very thinly, lay the slices out on the draining board and sprinkle with the salt. Leave for 30–40 minutes, then blot with paper towels.

Cook the potatoes for 15 minutes in boiling salted water.

Soften the onion in ⅓ cup of oil over low heat, then add the garlic.

Grease an earthenware dish or casserole (about 12 inches across and at least 3 inches deep) with oil. Make three layers of vegetables, starting with a third of the potato slices, then the eggplant slices, then the bell peppers, cooked onion, and garlic, together with some of the pan oil, plus parsley. Add 1 can of tomatoes and its juice, squeezing the tomatoes through clenched fingers to break them up well. Season with salt, pepper, and the paprika. Repeat until all the ingredients are in. Sprinkle vinegar over the second layer and 1–1½ tablespoons of oil over the top of the dish.

Cover with foil and bake for 1 hour. Remove the foil, turn down the heat to 325°F, and cook for a further 30–60 minutes, to brown and concentrate the juices. Excellent hot or cold, this dish also reheats well.

Ingredients

2 medium eggplants
salt and freshly ground black pepper
9 small potatoes, peeled and sliced
2 large onions, chopped
½ cup olive oil
2 garlic cloves, minced
2 large sweet green bell peppers, seeded and sliced
1 large red bell pepper, seeded and sliced
¾ cup chopped fresh parsley
3 x 14-oz cans tomatoes
2 tsp paprika
¼ cup red wine vinegar

Serves 4

anchovy potato salad

Another tasty tapas dish from Spain. Anchovy adds an interesting flavor to ordinary potato salad. This potato dish can be successfully served with fish or meat as a side dish, or as one of many tapas dishes to make up a meal.

Ingredients

1 lb potatoes, washed, peeled, and cut into even shapes
1 tsp puréed anchovies or anchovy essence
1¼ cups homemade mayonnaise
2 tsp chopped fresh parsley
½ tsp freshly ground black pepper

Place the potatoes in a pan of water and salt, bring to a boil, and simmer gently for about 10 minutes, or until just firm. Drain.

Blend the anchovy paste or essence into the mayonnaise with the parsley and black pepper; taste. If you want a stronger anchovy taste, add more anchovy paste or essence.

Carefully stir into the potatoes. Serve.

Ingredients

8-oz can black beans, drained
½ cup corn kernels, fresh, frozen, or canned and drained
8 oz ripe tomatoes, chopped
4 green onions, trimmed and chopped
½ sweet green bell pepper, seeded and finely diced
½ red bell pepper, seeded and finely diced
2 Tbsp olive oil
1 cup red wine vinegar
hot pepper sauce to taste
Worcestershire sauce to taste
ground cumin to taste
salt and freshly ground black pepper
1 star fruit, ½ diced, ½ sliced crosswise in thin sections

Serves 4

This is the perfect dish to accompany barbecued or broiled fish and poultry dishes.

mia-mex star fruit and black bean salsa

Mix the beans with the corn, tomatoes, onions, bell peppers, olive oil, and vinegar, and season to taste with the hot pepper sauce, Worcestershire sauce, cumin, and salt and pepper.

Stir the diced star fruit into the mixture and place the slices across the top.

Cover and refrigerate for at least 3 hours to allow the flavors to blend. Serve chilled.

Serves 4

The beauty of this dish is that it is so easy to prepare, yet looks company-worthy. Serve it with just about any entrée, or try serving it with one of the appetizers in this book to make a whole meal!

corn cubana

Ingredients

8 oz chorizo, cooked, casing removed, and finely chopped; or streaky bacon, cooked and crumbled
1 large onion, chopped
2 x 15-oz cans whole kernel sweetcorn, drained of all but 1 Tbsp juice
8-oz can tomato sauce
freshly ground black pepper

In a large skillet, fry the chorizo or bacon and onion together until the onions are tender. Set aside to cool.

Add 1 tablespoon of corn juice and tomato sauce to the meat drippings and cook slowly, stirring frequently, for about 1 hour. Season with the pepper to taste.

Add the corn and cook for 1 minute. Before serving, spread the chorizo or bacon over the top of the corn-tomato mixture.

Serves 4

Serve *piononos*, as this dish is known in Puerto Rico, with rice and garden peas or with rice and black beans.

deep-fried plantain rings with ground beef

Ingredients

2 large, ripe plantains
½ stick butter
2 tsp vegetable oil
2 Tbsp vegetable oil mixed with 1 tsp liquid annatto
1 lb lean ground beef
1 small onion, chopped
½ sweet green bell pepper, chopped
1 fresh hot pepper, chopped
1 garlic clove, minced
1 heaped Tbsp all-purpose flour
3 ripe tomatoes, skinned and chopped
3 Tbsp water
1 tsp salt
freshly ground black pepper
1½ Tbsp vinegar
4 eggs
vegetable oil

Peel the plantains. Heat the butter with the 2 teaspoons vegetable oil in a large skillet. Cut each plantain lengthwise into 4 thick slices. Cook them in the pan for 4 minutes, turning them over now and again until they have browned. Drain them on absorbent paper towels.

Heat the annatto-flavored oil in the same pan over medium heat, and add the beef, onion, green bell pepper, hot pepper, and garlic. Cook for 5 minutes.

Add the flour and stir it in, then add the tomatoes, water, salt, and freshly ground black pepper to taste. Cook until the mixture thickens. Stir in the vinegar.

To make the *piononos*, carefully bend each plantain slice around into a ring about 3 inches in diameter, securing the overlapping ends with a wooden toothpick. Lay the rings side by side.

Spoon the beef mixture into each ring, and press the tops as flat as possible.

Beat the eggs and brush some over the *piononos*.

Heat enough oil in a large pan to deep-fry the *piononos*. Fry them for about 3 minutes each side, turning them over very gently. Drain them on absorbent paper towels, and serve as soon as they are all cooked.

Serves 4

INGREDIENTS

8 small or 3 large tomatoes
4 hard-cooked eggs, cooled and peeled
¾ cup garlic mayonnaise
freshly ground black pepper
1 Tbsp chopped fresh parsley
1 Tbsp white bread crumbs for the large tomatoes
chopped fresh parsley for garnish

Tapas dishes are a gift to the vegetarian, since many contain no meat. This one is no exception. You can use small or large tomatoes for this recipe, which is very simple and a colorful addition to any table.

Skin the tomatoes, first by cutting out the core with a sharp knife and making a X-shaped incision on the other end of the tomato. Place in a pan of boiling water for 10 seconds, remove, and plunge into a bowl of iced or very cold water (this latter step is to stop the tomatoes from cooking and going mushy). Slip off the skins.

Slice the tops off the tomatoes, and just enough of their bases to remove the rounded ends so that the tomatoes will sit squarely on the plate. Keep the tops if using small tomatoes, but not for the large tomatoes.

Remove the seeds and insides, either with a teaspoon or a small, sharp knife.

Mash the eggs with the mayonnaise, salt, pepper, and the 1 tablespoon parsley.

Fill the tomatoes, firmly pressing down the filling. With small tomatoes, replace the lids at a jaunty angle. If keeping to serve later, brush them with olive oil and black pepper to prevent them from drying out. Cover with plastic wrap and keep in the refrigerator.

For large tomatoes, the filling must be very firm, so it can be sliced. If you make your own mayonnaise, thicken it by using more egg yolks. If you use store-bought mayonnaise, add enough white bread crumbs until the mixture is the consistency of mashed potatoes. Season well, to taste. Fill the tomatoes, pressing down firmly until level. Refrigerate for 1 hour, then slice with a sharp knife into rings. Sprinkle with chopped parsley.

COOK'S TIP

Making Mayonnaise

Remember when making mayonnaise that all ingredients should be at room temperature. Put 2 egg yolks in a bowl with ½ tsp salt and 1 tsp Dijon mustard and whisk together.

Beat constantly and evenly, adding ½ pint olive oil at a very slow trickle. When all the oil is added, you should have a thick, glossy emulsion that clings to the whisk.

Gradually beat in 2 tsp cider vinegar. For a thinner mayonnaise, beat in 1 Tbsp hot water.

Serves 4

Ingredients

2 large red bell peppers
2 large tomatoes
2 garlic cloves, minced
1 Tbsp chopped fresh marjoram
¼ cup olive oil
salt and freshly ground black pepper

The Spanish name of this recipe, *asadilla*, means "little baked vegetables," and this all-red salad is a summer favorite. It can be served with lightly toasted bread or decorated with anchovy strips.

red bell peppers and tomato baked salad

Skin the bell peppers. If you have gas, hold them on a carving fork in the flame, until they are black and blistered. Otherwise broil, giving them a quarter-turn every 5 minutes. Put them in a plastic bag for 10 minutes. Then strip off the skins on a plate. Pull out the stems and discard the seeds, but keep the juice.

Meanwhile, skin the tomatoes, quarter them, and turn their seeds and juice into a jug. Slice the flesh lengthwise into strips and put into an oiled baking dish.

Slice the bell peppers the same way and mix in. Sprinkle with the garlic, herbs, olive oil, and salt and pepper.

Press the tomato and bell pepper juices through a strainer, add them, and mix everything gently. Bake in a preheated oven (at the highest temperature possible) for about 20 minutes, then leave until cold.

This is delicious as a salad, but it can be puréed to make a sauce for chicken or fish.

Serves 4–6

If you have some leftover cooked rice on hand, this dish can be whipped up in just a few minutes with the help of a can opener and the chopping board. It makes a filling, nutritious accompaniment to any light main dish. For color, lay strips of pimento or red bell peppers across the top.

black bean and rice salad

Ingredients

- 2 cups cooked or canned black beans, rinsed and drained
- 2 cups cooked rice
- $1\frac{1}{2}$ cups fresh chopped cilantro
- $\frac{1}{4}$ cup lime juice
- $\frac{3}{4}$ cup oil
- $\frac{1}{2}$ cup chopped onion
- 2 garlic cloves, minced
- salt and freshly ground black pepper
- pimento or red bell pepper strips for garnish (optional)

Mix the beans, rice, and cilantro together in a bowl. Place the lime juice in a small bowl and whisk in the oil.

Then add the onion and garlic, and toss with the beans, combining the ingredients well.

Add salt and pepper to taste, and garnish with pimento or red bell pepper if wished. Serve at room temperature or chilled.

Serves 4

In this traditional recipe, vegetables were baked round the barbecue in summer and then dressed to serve cold. Here they are baked in the oven and make a good vegetarian main course. A variety of vegetables can be used–just adjust cooking times to suit them.

murcian salad of mixed baked vegetables

Ingredients

3 small eggplants (about 7 oz each)
3 sweet green bell peppers
4 medium onions, darkest skin removed
4 large tomatoes
1 bunch of spring garlic or fat green onions, tips trimmed
⅔ cup olive oil
3 garlic cloves, bruised
juice of 1 lemon
salt and freshly ground black pepper
⅓ cup chopped fresh parsley

Preheat the oven to 400°F. Put the eggplants, bell peppers, onions, tomatoes, trimmed spring garlic or green onions into 1–2 roasting pans with the oil and garlic cloves. A big pan will need about ½ cup of water to stop the juices burning.

Bake them for 25 minutes, then remove the tomatoes (you may also be able to combine pans at this point). After another 15 minutes, remove the bell peppers. Give the other vegetables a squeeze to see how close they are to being done. Put the bell peppers into a plastic bag, as this helps with the skinning later.

The eggplants will probably be ready in about another 15 minutes, but onions usually need another 15 minutes or more. Stir the juices in the roasting pan and pour them into a cup, discarding the garlic cloves.

Skin the tomatoes whole and arrange them in the center of a big platter, then just cut them across like a star. Skin the rest of the vegetables, slice them lengthwise, and keep all the juices they exude. Arrange the vegetables in sets on the platter, radiating around the tomatoes. Arrange the eggplants so their exotic seeds are upward.

Sprinkle lemon juice over the salad and season. Then stir the reserved pan juices, and dribble some into the center of the tomatoes and over the salad. Sprinkle with parsley and serve.

Serves 4–6

Ingredients

2 x 6½-oz cans white tuna in water, drained and flaked
1½ cups diced mango or papaya, drained well
1½ cups chopped celery
½ cup papaya seeds, ground to size of peppercorns (optional)
½ cup grated carrots
¼ cup chopped green onions
¼ cup chopped red onion
¾ cup mayonnaise
½ tsp curry powder
lettuce leaves

This dish is a symphony of flavors and textures, with mango and tuna as the stars. The curry brings everything together beautifully.

curried tuna salad with tropical fruit

Combine the tuna, mango or papaya, celery, papaya seeds if using, half the carrots, and green and red onions in a bowl.

Combine the mayonnaise and curry powder in a small bowl, then add to the tuna mixture and toss gently to mix. Cover and chill.

Spoon the salad into a lettuce-lined serving dish. Sprinkle the remaining carrot over the salad for garnish.

Serves 4

Ingredients

1 large fresh pineapple, or 16-oz can unsweetened pineapple, cut into bite-sized chunks, drained
2 lb crab meat, cut into chunks, or ocean sticks or crab sticks
1 large mango, peeled and cubed
8 oz orange-flesh melon balls
2 cups seedless grapes
yogurt or sour cream to serve (optional)

Ocean sticks or crab sticks work well in this salad because when it is served cold in a no-cook dish, the white-fish based dish is very similar to more expensive crab meat. Of course, if you prefer to use real crab meat, by all means do so.

fruited crab salad

Combine the pineapple, crab meat, ocean sticks, or crab sticks, mango, orange-flesh melon balls, and grapes. Place them in pineapple boats or in a glass bowl. Chill until ready to serve.

Serve with yogurt or sour cream, if desired.

Cook's Tip

If you are using fresh pineapple, cut it lengthwise into quarters, cutting through the crown, remove the fruit from the shells, discard the core, and reserve the shells to use as "pineapple boats."

Serves 4–6

A first-course salad is the common Spanish pattern and it may contain canned tuna and egg. This recipe for vinaigrette is really delicious.

mixed salad from madrid

Make the viniagrette. Mash the garlic on a board with a pinch of salt, working with the flat of a knife or in a mortar. In a bowl or the mortar with the garlic, stir in the vinegar, paprika, and pepper, then the oil.

To eat white onions raw, soak the rings in water for 10 minutes. Drain and blot dry. Line the base of a shallow salad bowl or platter with lettuce. Flake the tuna over it, decorate with the onion rings, sliced cooked eggs, and olives. Add the slices or wedges of tomato and the canned asparagus, if using. Sprinkle with some of the vinaigrette.

Ingredients

rings cut from the center of 1 Spanish onion, or 1 white onion, sliced
1 lettuce (Romaine or Iceberg), washed, dried, and chilled
7-oz can tuna, drained
2 hard-cooked eggs, peeled and sliced
½ cup *manzanilla* olives or other small green olives
2–3 tomatoes, (optional), sliced or cut into wedges
9-oz can white asparagus, drained (optional)

For Vinaigrette
1 garlic clove, finely chopped
¼ tsp salt
¼ cup sherry vinegar
pinch of paprika
freshly ground black pepper
scant ½ cup olive oil

Serves 6

INGREDIENTS

8 oz salt cod, soaked overnight and drained
juice of 1 lime or lemon
1 onion, finely chopped
3 tomatoes, chopped
3 Tbsp olive oil
2 hard-cooked eggs, chopped
1 fresh hot pepper, seeded and finely chopped
2 Tbsp finely chopped green onions
1 sweet green bell pepper, seeded and finely chopped
2 Tbsp finely chopped fresh parsley
freshly ground black pepper

Salt cod was originally brought to the Caribbean as food for slaves by the Colonists. Of all salted fish, cod seems to have the best flavor.

salt cod salad

Boil the cod for 20 minutes or until it flakes. Drain, and rinse, under cold running water. Remove the skin and bones, and flake the fish.

Put the flaked fish into a glass bowl, add the lime or lemon juice, onion, tomatoes, olive oil, eggs, hot pepper, green onions, bell pepper, parsley, and freshly ground black pepper, and mix well.

When the mixture has cooled, cover the bowl with plastic wrap and refrigerate overnight.

Serve the next day on crackers, fresh bread, or small, toasted slices of bread.

desserts and drinks

Serves 8

INGREDIENTS

5 medium, ripe mangoes
3 Tbsp lime or lemon juice
2 egg whites
pinch of salt
¼ cup sugar
6 Tbsp heavy cream

Make sure that you use ripe mangoes in this dish. The sweet, juicy flesh creates a deliciously smooth mousse.

Peel the mangoes and remove the flesh from the seeds. Dice the flesh of 2 of the mangoes, and purée the rest in a blender.

Put the purée into a glass mixing bowl, and stir in the lime or lemon juice.

Beat the egg whites with the salt until they are frothy. Sprinkle in the sugar, and continue to beat until stiff. Then gently fold in the cream.

Gradually stir the mixture into the mango purée. Pour over the diced mango. Spoon the mixture into serving bowls or glasses, and then chill for at least 3 hours before serving. If you wish, garnish with mango slices as shown here.

Serves 6

INGREDIENTS

FOR CARAMEL
¾ cup superfine sugar
1 Tbsp water

FLAN
4 small eggs
2 egg yolks
½ cup sweetened condensed milk
½ cup milk
¼ cup plus 2 tsp superfine sugar
8 oz fresh mango pulp or nectarines or peaches, puréed and strained

This recipe combines two great Cuban loves–flan and mango. Canned pulp may be substituted for fresh, if you are making it out of season.

Mix the sugar and water in a small saucepan and cook on medium-high heat, stirring often, until the mixture bubbles and turns a light caramel color. Pour the caramel into 6 ramekins. Gently tilt the ramekins to coat the sides with caramel. Set aside to cool.

Preheat the oven to 250°F. Add the eggs, egg yolks, condensed milk, milk, and the ¼ cup sugar to the fruit pulp, and blend thoroughly. Pour into the caramelized ramekins. Sprinkle the 2 teaspoons sugar over the ramekins.

Place the ramekins in a large roasting pan and pour simmering water into the pan so it comes halfway up the sides of the ramekins.

Bake for 40 minutes, or until a toothpick inserted in the center comes out clean. Chill before inverting to serve.

Right: Mango mousse

Serves 8

This very old recipe for *flaò* is made all round the Mediterranean, and appears in the first cookbook printed in Spain in the fifteenth century.

sweet cheesecake with mint

Ingredients

4 small eggs
¼ cup clear honey
⅔ cup superfine sugar
2⅓ cups soft full-fat cream cheese
15 fresh mint leaves
1 Tbsp dry anis or anisette (or Pernod)
confectioners' sugar for dusting

For Pastry

1½ cups all-purpose flour, plus extra for rolling
pinch of salt
½ stick chilled butter, diced, plus extra for greasing
1 small egg
1 tsp dry anis or anisette (or Pernod)
1½–2 Tbsp milk

Make the pastry. Sift the flour and salt into a food processor or bowl. Cut in the fat, then beat in the egg and anis or anisette, adding enough milk to make a dough. Pull the pastry together into a ball and chill for 15 minutes.

Preheat the oven to 325°F and place a heavy baking sheet in it to warm.

Make the filling. Beat the eggs, honey, and sugar together. Work in the cream cheese, mint leaves, and anis or anisette.

Roll out the pastry on a floured surface. Roll it round a rolling pin and lift this over a greased quiche pan, 10 inches in diameter, with a removable bottom. Fit the pastry into the pan. Pour in the filling, smooth the top, and bake on the baking sheet for 40–50 minutes, until slightly risen and golden.

Leave to cool for 5 minutes, then remove the flan ring. Chill well.

You can make fancy decorations on top with more fresh mint leaves, but all it needs is a dusting with some confectioners' sugar.

Serves 8

White chocolate combines perfectly with coconut in this rich tart. You will need a double boiler for best results.

white chocolate coconut tart

Preheat the oven to 400°F. Follow the package directions for unfolding the crust into a 9 x 1 inch round tart pan with a removable bottom. Fold the excess crust into the pan, pressing it firmly against sides and making crust even with top of pan. Prick bottom and sides with a fork.

Line the shell with kitchen foil and fill it with dry beans or rice. Place it on a baking sheet and bake on the lowest oven rack for 15 minutes. Remove the foil and beans and return to the oven to bake until browned and fully baked, which should take about 12 more minutes. Remove from the oven and place on a wire rack to cool.

In the top of double boiler, combine the cornstarch and sugar. Whisk in the egg yolks until smooth. Stir in the rum and 4 tablespoons of water. Cook over simmering water, whisking constantly and vigorously, for about 15–20 minutes, until the mixture is very thick and smooth. Do not boil.

Remove the pan from the water. Stir in the butter until combined, then pour into a medium-size bowl. Let cool, cover, and place in the refrigerator.

Clean the top of the double boiler, then over simmering water, melt together the remaining 2 tablespoons of water and the chocolate, stirring occasionally, until smooth. Remove from the heat and whisk the chocolate into the rum mixture. Let cool, then cover and refrigerate until cold.

Fold the unsweetened coconut and whipped cream into the rum mixture, and pour into tart shell. Refrigerate for at least 2 hours.

Ingredients

1 sheet of shortcrust pastry, thawed if frozen
2 tsp cornstarch
2 Tbsp sugar
4 egg yolks
2 Tbsp dark rum
6 Tbsp water
½ stick unsalted butter, softened
8 oz white chocolate, chopped
7 heaped Tbsp shredded unsweetened coconut
¾ cup heavy cream, whipped
3 heaped Tbsp shredded sweetened coconut, toasted, for garnish
white chocolate curls for garnish, pared from a white chocolate bar (optional)

Serves 4–6

INGREDIENTS

vanilla ice cream
3 Tbsp butter
3 Tbsp brown sugar
½ tsp ground cinnamon
3 Tbsp rum, orange liqueur, or orange juice
2 medium bananas, ripe but still firm, peeled and diced

This is called Banana Salsa because the bananas are chopped and cooked with seasonings, but it's really a sort of chopped Bananas Foster, served over ice cream.

banana salsa

Have someone spoon the ice cream into serving dishes while you are preparing the Banana Salsa, because it cooks quickly.

Melt the butter over low heat in a medium skillet. Stir in the brown sugar and cinnamon until dissolved.

Add the rum, liqueur, or orange juice, and stir for about 30 seconds. Add the bananas, cook for about 1 minute, until the bananas have softened slightly. Spoon over the ice cream and serve immediately.

Serves 6

This dessert is served in the south of Spain as a special treat for invalids and children. It was taken to Paris by Eugenia de Montijo where it became *riz l'impératrice*. It is normally dusted with cinnamon, but can be decorated with mandarin segments or grapes.

andalusian creamy chilled rice

INGREDIENTS

- ¼ cup short-grain rice
- 5¾ cups milk
- 1 vanilla bean, split in 2
- 1 good cup superfine sugar
- 6 egg yolks
- ground cinnamon
- 2 lemons
- 1 cup heavy cream

Wash the rice in a strainer under running water. Tip it into a pan of boiling water and cook for 5 minutes, then drain well.

Heat generous 2 cups of milk in a pan and add the rice, half the vanilla bean, and ⅓ cup of sugar. Simmer for about 25 minutes, until the rice has expanded and the mixture is thick. Cream the egg yolks with the remaining sugar in a heatproof bowl that fits over a pan of simmering water.

Heat the remaining milk and pour it into the egg and sugar mixture, adding the rest of the vanilla bean. Cook gently, stirring, until the custard coats the back of a spoon, then remove the vanilla bean. Stir the rice into the custard with a pinch of cinnamon and leave until cold.

Cut 6 round discs of peel from the side of the lemons. Blanch them in boiling water for 2 minutes, then drain and refresh them under cold running water. Whip the cream and fold it into the rice.

Turn into a shallow bowl and push the lemon peel into the rice at regular intervals. Chill well. Before serving, dust cinnamon over the top as a final touch.

Serves 6–8

The Spanish name, *Leche Frita*, means fried milk, and the reason this dessert is so popular all along the north coast of Spain is that is combines a melting creamy center with a crunchy coating. Eat them hot or cold.

galician crisp custard squares

Ingredients

2¼ cups creamy milk
3 strips of lemon zest
½ cinnamon stick
scant ½ cup superfine sugar, plus extra for dusting
⅓ cup cornstarch
3 Tbsp flour
3 large egg yolks
sunflower oil for frying
2 eggs for coating
½–⅔ cup bread crumbs (or dried crumbs)
ground cinnamon

Bring the milk, the lemon zest, cinnamon stick, and sugar to a boil in a saucepan, stirring gently. Cover and leave off the heat to infuse for 20 minutes.

Put the cornstarch and flour in a bowl and beat in the egg yolks with a wooden spoon. Start adding some of the milk until the batter is smooth. Strain in the rest of the hot milk, then pour back into the pan. Cook over low heat, stirring continuously—it will not curdle, but it does thicken unevenly if you let it. Cook for a couple of minutes until it becomes a thick custard that separates from the side of the pan. Beat it hard with the spoon to keep it smooth. Pour into a small baking pan, smoothing to a square about 7–8 inches and about ½ inch deep. Cool and then chill.

Pour oil into a shallow skillet to a depth of about ½ inch and heat until very hot. Cut the custard into 8–12 squares. Beat the eggs on a plate and lift half of the squares with a spatula into the egg. Coat and then lift them onto a tray of crumbs (big stale crumbs are best, but dried will do) and coat all round.

Lift the squares with a clean spatula into the oil and fry for a couple of minutes, shaking or spooning the oil over the top, until golden. Reserve on paper towels while you fry the second batch. Dust with sugar and cinnamon before serving. They can be served hot, but are even better well chilled.

This pudding, a favorite at Key West's Palm Grill, combines the love Cuban-Americans have for *café con leche*–espresso coffee laced with steaming milk and sugar–with their love of custard. It makes an exotic, decorative change to normal mid-morning coffee, and is perfect for a special occasion.

Serves 4

café con leche custard

Ingredients

- 4 Tbsp cornstarch
- scant 3 cups milk
- 1 cup heavy cream
- 2½ Tbsp instant coffee granules
- 1⅛ cups sugar
- 2 eggs
- whipped cream for garnish
- chocolate-covered espresso beans for garnish

Stir the cornstarch into 1 cup of milk, stirring until smooth. In the top of a double boiler, place all the remaining ingredients, except the eggs and garnish, and stir in the cornstarch mixture. Stir over medium-high heat until the mixture thickens. Cover and simmer for 10 minutes.

Beat the eggs well. Slowly add 1 cup of the hot coffee mixture to the eggs, beating continually. Pour the egg mixture into the remaining coffee mixture in the double boiler, still over heat, and beat well to incorporate. Cover and simmer for 2 minutes.

Remove from the heat and pour into coffee cups. Cover with plastic wrap, cool, and then refrigerate.

When chilled, top with fresh whipped cream and a chocolate-covered espresso bean.

Serves 10

When you are sitting out under the trees at night, waiting for the first breath of cooler air after a long, hot day, nothing is as refreshing as a lemon *granizado*.

iced lemonade-sorbet

Wash the lemons and pare the zest from them with a potato peeler. Halve them, squeeze out the juice and reserve it. Put the zest in a bowl and pour the boiling water over it. Leave until cold.

Remove the zest and stir in the sugar and lemon juice. Leave to stand and stir again after 5 minutes, checking the sugar has dissolved. Keep it in a bottle in the fridge.

To serve, pour the lemonade into a jug and add an equal amount of water. Fill tall glasses with ice slush, pour the liquid over it, and drink through straws.

Ingredients

5 juicy lemons
2¼ cups boiling water
¾ cups sugar
2¼ cups cold water
10 glasses of ice slush

Serves 4

This type of Creole drink is now popular in the West, where frozen yogurt is typically used. It combines a delicious medley of fruits.

tropical fruit smoothies

Combine the orange juice, sugar, and lime juice, and pour into an 8-inch square baking pan. Freeze until firm.

Break the frozen juice mixture into chunks. Place the juice chunks, fruit, fruit spread, and vanilla extract in a blender or food processor, and process until smooth.

Pour into glasses and serve immediately, decorated with lime, kiwi, or orange slices, or a sprig of mint, if desired.

Ingredients

2 cups unsweetened orange juice or frozen yogurt
2 Tbsp confectioners' sugar
2 Tbsp fresh lime juice
2 cups sliced fresh strawberries, raspberries, peaches, nectarines, banana, mango, papaya, guava
3 Tbsp complementary no-sugar-added fruit spread, such as strawberry, peach, orange marmalade
1 tsp vanilla extract
4 lime or orange slices or sprigs of mint (optional)

Serves 10

This unusual, delicately spiced drink hails from the Caribbean, where its refreshing flavor is a great accompaniment to long, hot days.

Ingredients

1 lb fresh sorrel leaves or ¼ lb dry
2 bay leaves
3 whole cloves
1 small cinnamon stick
4 cups white sugar

Put the sorrel and bay leaves, cloves, cinnamon, and sugar into a large saucepan. Pour over hot water to cover the leaves and boil for 1 minute only.

Remove the pan from the heat and leave to cool. Let the pan stand overnight.

Next day, strain out the leaves and spices and sweeten to taste, if necessary. Bottle and put 1 whole clove in each bottle. Cap the bottles and leave to stand for 4 days. Chill and serve with ice cubes.

cakes and cookies

Makes 12 cups

These cookie cups are light and elegant. Although the individual components can be made early in the day, the salsa should not be added until just before serving time.

cookie cups with ricotta cream and fruit salad

Ingredients

- ½ cup toasted pine nuts
- 3 Tbsp butter at room temperature
- ⅓ cup sugar
- ½ tsp vanilla extract
- 3 egg whites
- ¼ tsp ground cinnamon
- ⅛ tsp salt
- 5 Tbsp all-purpose flour
- about 1 cup dessert fruit salsa of your choice

For Ricotta Cream

- ½ cup heavy cream
- ½ tsp vanilla extract
- ½ cup ricotta cheese
- ½ cup confectioners' sugar

Preheat the oven to 375°F. Grind the toasted pine nuts to crumbs in a food processor, taking care not to let them turn to paste. Set aside.

Line 2 cookie sheets with parchment or wax paper. Have ready an ungreased 12-cup muffin pan.

Cream together the butter, sugar, and vanilla extract, then add the egg whites, cinnamon, and salt, and beat until the mixture is smooth. Add the ground pine nuts and flour, and mix by hand until smooth again.

Drop tablespoonfuls of the batter onto the prepared cookie sheets, 4 inches apart. With a rubber spatula, spread the batter into thin, 3-inch circles. Bake for about 4 minutes, until the cookies are firm and have just started to brown around the edges. Because you have to work fast with baked cookies, it is best to bake one sheet at a time.

As soon as the cookies are done, remove them from the oven. With a wide metal spatula, carefully remove each warm cookie from the sheet and gently press it into muffin cup so that it forms a cup. The crimped edges do not need to be uniform. Work quickly so that you get all the cookies into the muffin pan while they are still warm, otherwise, they will crack. Repeat with the second sheet of cookies. Let the cookies cool in the muffin pan. (Note: If it is a humid day, the cookies will not get crisp, so leave them in the muffin pan until serving time.)

Make the ricotta cream. Beat the heavy cream with the vanilla extract until soft peaks form. In another bowl, beat together the ricotta cheese and confectioners' sugar. Fold in the whipped cream. Refrigerate until ready to use.

Divide the ricotta cream among the cookie cups. This is best done no more than 2 hours before serving time, so that the cookies do not become soggy. Immediately before serving, top each cup with a tablespoon or so of fruit salsa.

Cook's Tip

To toast pine nuts, spread them on a cookie sheet. Bake at 350°F for 5–10 minutes until golden-brown, watching them carefully, as they burn easily.

Makes about 20

Sopapillas, little pillows of deep-fried pastry dough, are traditionally served with honey, or sprinkled with cinnamon and confectioners' sugar. For a new twist, try stuffing them with a dessert salsa.

sopapillas

Ingredients

- 2 cups all-purpose flour
- 2 tsp baking powder
- ½ tsp salt
- 3 Tbsp solid shortening
- vegetable oil for frying
- ground cinnamon
- confectioners' sugar
- 1½ cups dessert salsa

Mix the flour, baking powder, and salt together in a bowl. Cut the shortening into the flour mixture until it resembles fine bread crumbs. Add ¾ cup water and knead until it forms a stiff dough, a little moister and more elastic than pie crust dough. Seal in plastic wrap and let rest for about 30 minutes.

On a floured board, roll out half the dough to a thickness of ⅛ inch. Cut out 3-inch squares. Gather up the scraps, combine with the remaining dough, and repeat.

Pour vegetable oil into a deep skillet to a depth of 1–2 inches. Heat to 375°F. The temperature is important because if it is too cold, the sopapillas will be greasy; while if it is too hot, the outside of the sopapillas will brown before the inside is cooked.

Put a few squares of dough in the hot oil. They should not touch. Cook until puffy and golden-brown, turning once, about 1 minute for each side. Remove and drain on paper towels. Let the oil return to 375°F between batches.

Dust the sopapillas with cinnamon and confectioners' sugar, before cutting a slit along one edge and stuffing with a spoonful of dessert salsa.

Makes 8–10

INGREDIENTS

2 cups all-purpose flour
2 Tbsp butter
½ tsp salt
2 tsp baking powder
2 tsp sugar
⅔ cup milk

These are the Creole version of a biscuit, fried in hot oil, and variations of this recipe are eaten throughout the Caribbean as a delicious snack. Make a big batch–they go fast!

Sift the dry ingredients into a bowl, then cut in the butter with a knife until the mixture resembles bread crumbs. Pour in the milk and stir to make a soft dough.

Knead on a floured board for about 5 minutes, then refrigerate for 30 minutes.

Break the dough into lemon-sized pieces, roll these into balls and flatten to a thickness of ½ inch. Fry these in hot oil until they are golden.

Serves 3–4

Made with milk, these are a popular home-from-school treat for children in central Spain. Made with wine, however, they are good enough for adults. French bread looks more elegant than any other.

sugared toasts

Heat the oil in a skillet and, when ready to fry, dip the bread rounds into milk or wine on each side and then into beaten egg.

Fry on both sides, briefly, until crisp and golden. Drain on paper towels.

Serve hot, generously sprinkled with sugar and cinnamon.

Ingredients

8 thick slices of stale French bread
½ scant cup milk or red wine
2 eggs, beaten
⅓ cup sunflower oil
sugar for sprinkling
pinch of ground cinnamon

Makes about 20

In Spain children eat these hazelnut macaroons with a glass of milk for *merienda* at the end of the afternoon.

hazelnut macaroons

Preheat the oven to 375°F, and while it heats toast the nuts in the oven for about 20 minutes. Grind them (if you use a food processor, do not over-grind them so that they start to turn oily).

Rub some sugar over the grater to pick up leftover lemon oil and then rub the zest well into all the sugar. Sprinkle with cinnamon.

Beat the egg whites until soft peaks form, and then stir about a quarter of the whites into the ground nuts to soften them. Sprinkle about half the sugar over the whites and gently fold in, then fold in the remainder alternately with the nut mixture.

Dot walnut-sized pieces onto greased foil on 1 or 2 cookie sheets, pressing them out gently and spacing them 1 inch apart. Bake for 15 minutes until golden-brown. Let cool for 5 minutes, then remove from the foil.

Ingredients

1¼ cups blanched hazelnuts
⅔ cup superfine sugar
finely grated zest of
½ lemon
pinch of ground cinnamon
2 large egg whites
butter for greasing

sweet potato flapjacks

Serves 6

Sweet potatoes are a common ingredient in Caribbean cuisine. Here used in a sweet dish, they are equally useful eaten as a vegetable.

INGREDIENTS

1 lb sweet potatoes
1½ sticks butter
½ tsp salt
1 cup firmly packed light brown sugar
2 eggs
½ tsp freshly grated nutmeg
½ tsp ground ginger
2 Tbsp rum

Preheat the oven to 350°F. Peel and grate the sweet potatoes. Set aside until required.

Cream the butter with the salt and gradually blend in the sugar. Beat until light and fluffy.

Add the eggs, nutmeg, ginger, rum, and grated sweet potato, mixing well. Spoon the mixture into a greased baking dish, smooth the top, and bake in the preheated oven for 1 hour.

Let cool, then cut it into slices. Serve with rum-flavored whipped cream.

Makes 2 loaves

Sweet corn bread is a Caribbean bake, from the Dominican Republic. It's a great staple, full of taste and very nutritious.

sweet corn bread

Preheat the oven to 400°F. Use 1 tablespoon of the butter to grease two 7 x 4 x 3 inch bread pans. Shake a little flour in each pan to coat.

Sift the remaining flour, cornmeal, baking powder, cinnamon, nutmeg, and cloves together. Gradually mix in the coconut milk and milk.

Cream the remaining butter with the sugar until it is light and fluffy. Beat in the eggs, one at a time. Gradually incorporate the cornmeal mixture and coconut.

Pour the batter into the prepared pans, and bake in the center of the preheated oven for 35 minutes or until golden-brown.

Leave to cool in the pans for 5 minutes, then turn the loaves out onto wire racks to cool completely.

Ingredients

1¼ sticks plus 1 Tbsp butter
1¼ cups all-purpose flour
1¾ cups yellow cornmeal
2 tsp baking powder
½ tsp ground cinnamon
½ tsp freshly grated nutmeg
½ tsp ground cloves
⅓ cup coconut milk
⅓ cup milk
¼ cup sugar
4 eggs
1¼ cups grated fresh coconut

index